Praise for Te

MW00697991

"In his new book, *Teach Me, Teacher*, Jacob Chastain takes us on a transformational journey where past and present converge into possibility. His story of resilience and hope is a celebration of the impact each of us can have when professional purpose leads the way. Through twenty-two lessons, we begin to envision the immense potential for change as we contemplate a learning day fueled by joy–both ours and theirs."

—**Dr. Mary Howard**, author of *Good to Great Teaching*

"*Teach Me, Teacher* is one of the most courageous, heartbreaking, hopeful books I've ever read. By sharing his traumatic life stories and the lessons learned for how to live a better life, Jacob Chastain inspires us to be noble teachers for all our students. Written with grace, humility, empathy, and wisdom, the author shows how caring and compassionate teachers saved his life and inspired him to see life's possibilities. Every educator needs to read this book!

If this book is anything, it's proof of great teachers making an impact by simply modeling a better life. 'By being kind, they model a world in which smiles, good manners, and relentless support are normal. By being disciplined, they model a world in which we don't just mindlessly consume everything in sight but consciously choose where to concentrate our efforts. By being passionate, they model a world in which it's okay to dream big and reach for those damn stars above us.'"

—**Regie Routman**, author of *Literacy Essentials*

"Jacob Chastain pours his heart out on the pages of *Teach Me, Teacher* by sharing his personal journey through childhood trauma. His message that 'action is the antidote to suffering' is a powerful reminder to us all to do more, be more, understand more, and care more for our students."

—**Kim Bearden,** cofounder and executive director,
The Ron Clark Academy, author of *Talk to Me*

"Jacob Chastain's raw honesty is something that we need more of in the education world. In *Teach Me, Teacher*, he reflects on his past experiences while reminding us all how we can better serve our students and schools right where we are and because of who we are. His passion continues to inspire me and countless other educators to bring light and love into our classrooms every day."

—**Halee Sikorski**, elementary educator, A Latte Learning

"Everyone has their past, and Jacob's had challenges. At times raw and emotional, this book allows you to experience Jacob's journey towards understanding, acceptance, and redemption. Jacob shares example after example of how negatives in life can open doors, and his experiences can help the reader to better define a sense of purpose."

—**Evan Robb**, author of *The Ten-Minute Principal* and coauthor of *TeamMakers*

"My heart bled for children of shattered and dysfunctional families when I read Jacob Chastain's *Teach Me, Teacher*. Jacob has an insight many of us don't inherently have as teachers. His powerful story is a reminder that as teachers, we can and do make major impacts in the lives of our students. I applaud Jacob's willingness to be open and share his story. His book is filled with life lessons for us all, both in and out of the classroom."

—**Haley Curfman**, elementary educator, The Weary Teacher

"Jacob Chastain has done something that is extremely difficult—he has shared parts of his abusive childhood as well as his teaching experiences to show how he transformed negatives into positives to create a meaningful life, start his own family, and become a reflective teacher who responds to his students' needs. By sharing his painful memories, Jacob teaches us how to move away from them and focus on helping others. And that's exactly what he does every day in the classroom and through his outstanding podcasts with educators. By sharing his story, Jacob invites us to reflect on our stories in order to learn about life, relationships, teaching, and learning."

—**Laura Robb**, coauthor of *TeamMakers*

"By sharing his own challenging upbringing, Jacob Chastain offers a tribute to those teachers who supported and inspired him, while also reminding us that we may not know the trauma our students bring to our classrooms, even when they seem to be ok. *Teach Me, Teacher* is both an uplifting memoir and a message to all of us in education of the power we have to build relationships and make a difference for ALL of our students."

— Dr. Sue Szachowicz, senior fellow, Successful Practices Network, former principal, Brockton High School

"Jacob bares his soul in *Teach Me, Teacher* with a personal memoir that shares life-changing moments that have crafted who he is today. The story becomes even more powerful when he describes the impact of his teachers and how they provided him with safety and love when he needed it the most. This book is a must-read for all those who know a child who is going through challenging times."

—Adam Dovico, principal, Moore Magnet ES, author of *The Limitless School* and *Inside the Trenches*

"We know many of us—students and teachers—have experienced trauma. By sharing his own vulnerability, Jacob Chastain urges us to do better—for our kids, colleagues, and the world. *Teach Me, Teacher* is a desperate plea to make our classrooms and schools safe and accepting places of refuge."

—Jeff Anderson, author of *Patterns of Power, 10 Things Every Writer Needs to Know, Mechanically Inclined, Zack Delacruz, Just My Luck,* and *Upstaged*

"*Teach Me, Teacher* is essential guidance for the next generation of educators. It speaks to all of us—seasoned and green—with warmth and inescapable truths. Jacob Chastain shares his personal journey and thoughtfully connects it with the daily happenings of the classroom, reminding us that every single child we teach has their own story with a past, present, and future. The highly relatable lessons are told with a freshness and honesty unique to Jacob. *Teach Me, Teacher* is a great addition to every educator's bookshelf!"

—Marie Morris, high school ELA teacher, The Caffeinated Classroom

"Get ready for a journey that will make you laugh, cry, smile, and appreciate life and the amazing opportunity you have to impact the lives of your students. Jacob digs deep here, sharing stories that delve into his soul and the life that has made him the incredible educator (and person) he is today. Through his storytelling, you'll not only find inspiration but also practical mindset shifts and changes you can make today. Jacob shows us how to embrace negatives as positives, see the opportunities to make an impact even in seemingly bleak moments, and the power we have to use our passion, energy, and roles to change the lives of others. I suspect we'll begin to see *Teach Me, Teacher* at the top of must-read lists for years to come."

—Jeff Gargas, COO/cofounder,
Teach Better Team (teachbetter.com)

"I have followed Jacob Chastain on social media for years and he is the real deal. I was so excited when I found out he was writing *Teach Me, Teacher*, and I must say it does *not* disappoint. You'll want to join Jacob again and again as he not only shares his own story but also shares great ideas and resources along the way. I couldn't put this book down, and I bet you won't be able to either!"

—Todd Nesloney, award-winning author and
educator #KidsDeserveIt

"Jacob has found a way to harness the energy of teachers all across the country! His lessons sum up the importance of education and the promising future of the field. This book displays the kind of pride in education we need!"

—Esther Brunat, high school educator

Teach Me, Teacher

Life Lessons That Taught Me How to Be a Better Teacher

Jacob Chastain

Teach Me, Teacher
© 2019 by Jacob Chastain

This book is available at special discounts when purchased in quantity for use as premiums, promotions, fundraisers, or for educational use. For inquiries and details, contact the publisher at books@daveburgessconsulting.com.

Published by Dave Burgess Consulting, Inc.
San Diego, CA
DaveBurgessConsulting.com

Editing, cover design, and interior design by My Writers' Connection

Library of Congress Control Number: 2019944454
Paperback ISBN: 978-1-949595-46-8
Ebook ISBN: 978-1-949595-47-5

First Printing: July 2019

To the teachers who show up everyday
for their students.

Contents

Let It Rain

The home I grew up in was filled with tension. Thick, disgusting tension. The air was saturated with it.

My gut would tighten when it became too much. Physical fights and screaming matches rattled my mind, shaking my identity and leaving it fragile.

Anxiety filled me as I wondered why my mom couldn't finish her dinner. I would watch her head hang loosely over her plate, her fork wobbling in the air with a single green bean dancing delicately on its tip. When her pill-induced haze was in full swing, her drooping eyelids gave the impression that she was either dying or in bliss.

During these moments, I would be on the couch eating my own dinner and watching television, my father close by. I'd look over to her, and regardless of how old I was or how accustomed to the scene I had become, the tightness in my gut would return. I would inevitably feel sick, nervously rub my tongue on my teeth, and ride the rest of the night with a headache.

Today I wonder how many times I witnessed that scene. How many times did I see it before my father felt the need to tell his clever lies about it, the lies that made it seem as if she found the pills on her own, that he wasn't feeding them to her, and that they both didn't have the same addiction?

I wonder how many times I had to see it.

One night I felt the tightness, the sickness, and the headache, but I didn't think much of it because I had a new game to play. I had it all set up. My PlayStation 2 was hooked up to the big screen in the living room. I had snacks. It was going to be a good night. My sister and her friend were out with my mom somewhere. My brother was off with friends. My father was in the back of *his* house, in *his* room, watching *his* television.

Later I was at his door. I don't remember why. Maybe I was asking for something. I saw his face, and instantly my entire body was writhing in the boiling tension of the house. Something was different. He was mad at something, at me, at everything. My body reacted, but I was used to the feeling at that point. I was ten years old.

"I'll knock your head off!" he yelled.

I've heard this specific threat echo in my mind, in my dreams, so many times over the course of my life, though my father only made it once. I don't know why he shouted it at me.

To be honest, I remember being fiery with him. A smartass. We had an argument about this or that. I wasn't one to just sit there and take it. I stood up and said what I wanted to say. It was my best defense, a rickety wall that I cobbled together from fear and anger and confusion. I stood behind it, desperately hoping my bravado was enough to ride out the sick feeling in my body.

"I'll knock your head off!"

I stood there, unsure if it would actually happen. I played the odds.

"Go ahead!" I yelled back. For a moment, I thought he would. Then my mom came home.

My sister, well into her teens by then, wanted to get drunk that night. My mom figured it would be alright, of course, and came inside to ask my father for some money for the booze. He controlled the money with an iron fist.

A little later, I heard them screaming at each other.

Fighting.

Yelling.

Tension.

Normal.

I went back to my game.

Then the evening took a turn from bad to worse. Something changed. Things must have been said. I was up again and marching down the hall to their bedroom. I was the peacekeeper. I put myself in the middle of every fight, every issue, everything.

I collided with the wall as my mom pushed past me screaming and crying. I tried to say something to her, but my father was coming now like a train of fury, his legs and back stiff with age. Blind rage covered his face. He moved past me, and I followed, screaming and screaming and screaming. Following and screaming.

I watched as my life began to fall apart. I watched him grab her and throw her. My mom's head jerked, and her glasses bounced off her ears as she flew into the couch. He backed away and put his hands on his knees, waiting, stalking, toying with her.

"Stop!" I screamed. "Dad, stop, please!"

He pointed at me, eyes locking with mine. "Shut up!"

As I turned to run out of the house, I caught a glimpse of him as he charged at her with his fist clenched, ready to strike.

It was dark outside, and I was still screaming. I remember screaming to the sky. The stars watched in silence above me.

Then I screamed for my sister who had been waiting in the car for Mom to return with the money.

My sister found me and asked what was wrong. When I told her, I immediately knew we should run to my friend's house just down the street and ask for help. I tried to pull along her and her friend (who was nervously hanging back), but my sister wasn't having it. She ran back into the house to save our mom. I started running barefoot to my friend's house with my sister's friend behind me.

When they let me into the house, I was exhausted and crying. I could barely speak. My sister's friend explained what was going on as my friend's mom called the police. They asked her to ask me some questions, and I did the best I could to answer. Minutes later, my sister was crying on the porch holding her chest and her legs where my father had hit her.

The cop who arrived at my friend's house brought a brief moment of calm to the night. He was nice and understanding. Clearly good at talking to kids in stressful situations. I remember talking a lot to him as we walked towards my house (my father had already been hauled off to jail). I talk when I get nervous, or excited, or when I'm trying to work through my thoughts. Verbal processing and all. I remember telling him what happened as if it were an action movie, rather than the terrible thing it was.

His partners were equally nice and good with kids. They made us laugh. If I had the chance today, I would thank them. As a teacher now, I know what they were doing was invaluable and was essentially the only thing they could have done that would have helped in that moment. They listened. They talked. They smiled. They were present.

Trauma isn't an easy thing to get over, and many people struggle with it for the rest of their lives. Teachers see this. I've seen this. I've experienced this. When any of us face these moments in our classrooms, our schools, or our lives, we must do what we can.

Those police officers did, and it helped.

Back at my house my father was gone, but my mom was there, shaking in the corner and making necessary phone calls to arrange for us to leave. She shook so hard that it was like she had ice water coursing through her veins. I was standing in the living room. I asked her what my father did. What I had seen and what I could believe were two very different realities. She cried as she mimicked the sides of his fists colliding with her head and breaking her glasses. She sobbed uncontrollably and shook, and I looked at my paused video game on the television.

A few months later, I was back at my school after spending time at my grandma's house out in the country. I met with my fourth-grade teacher, Mrs. Urban, and she took me to a special table in the back of the room. The rest of the class was hard at work on something they had started the day before.

Some of what she told me that day has been lost to time, but I know the first thing she said was how glad she was that I was back in her classroom. She said so with a wonderful smile on her face, as always. The second thing she told me was the single most influential gift I ever received.

Mrs. Urban held up her hand in a fist, high above her head. She smiled, her glasses hanging slightly lower than her eyes so that she peered over them at me.

"This is a cloud," she said. She wiggled her fingers a little, a twinkle in her eye. "Now, whenever you have anything bad happen or you are thinking about something bad or something that makes you unhappy, put it in this little cloud so it's far away from you."

I remember thinking how stupid the whole thing was. *A cloud? Really? That's the best you got, lady?*

"Not forever, of course," she added. "Clouds can't hold rain all day." She smiled and dropped her hand. "But they can until we're nice and prepared for it."

At first, I didn't really understand what she meant. I didn't realize how amazing her words were until much later. Yet even without fully understanding, I started putting stuff in that cloud. Little by little, as I needed, I added to it.

I worry that some people will read this and think all Mrs. Urban did was teach me to bottle up my feelings, but that is not the case. She gave me permission to not be strong enough to deal with everything at once.

That cloud saved my life. It gave me a chance.

Truth be told, Mrs. Urban set me on a path that eventually led me back to her to let her know I had become a teacher myself. She was one of many teachers who saved my life over and over again and gave me the passion to reach out and be there for students the way they had been there for me.

That cloud, however, has grown darker through the years. It's heavy with memories and fragments of memories, sudden realizations, and a host of other experiences I've shoved inside it. It's grown dark, and it looks a lot like rain.

◇◇◇

My story and the stories of my students aren't written in this book to provide you with an opportunity for distant voyeurism into the world of trauma and fear. They are here as an encouragement to stop and reflect, as much for me as I hope they are for you. Many of the stories and truths in this book aren't easy to digest, but I believe they are necessary to face and understand for anyone who works with children or teenagers.

As educators, we must always attempt to grow, learn how to respond to the needs of the young minds in our classrooms, and use the life lessons we learn through our own experiences and the experiences of our students to determine how we can make the best possible difference in their lives. I've tried to model this practice throughout this book, and it's my hope that the intentions behind what I share in the pages that follow shine through to you, the reader. This is not a book sharing my personal gossip; it is a testimony to the power of teachers and the role they play in the lives of children all over the world.

— Lesson 2 —

Live in Truth

Growing up in a home filled with lies layered upon lies gave me an insatiable desire for truth. Nearly everything I believed as a child was at some point revealed to be a lie later in my life.

I grew up thinking my family was wealthy. I had the latest toys and game systems, and our Christmas tree—at least until I was about twelve—was always surrounded by gifts. It was all a lie, however, bought on shaky credit. That house of cards crumbled, leaving my illusions inside the home that was taken back by the banks.

I also grew up thinking my family involved me in every problem because they respected my intellect so much. I knew about the mounting bills as the credit began to run out, and about the drug problems of everyone in the house (which changed depending on the year), and I often served as the peacekeeper when arguments escalated to screaming matches. My mom would praise me, calling me the "preacher boy" as I preached to my family about how to fix their issues—a fact I now find disturbing.

It was all a lie. It wasn't respect for my intellect. It was irresponsible mental abuse of a child who wasn't old enough to deal with the issues plaguing the adults in his life. I still remember the face of my best friend's mother when I casually mentioned the financial troubles in my house. I thought it was normal small talk for a child, but she couldn't believe a kid knew about such family issues. I didn't understand why she was so angry about the whole thing.

Today, as a father, I can't imagine putting that kind of stress on my child. It actually makes me sick to think about and angry that I was never given a choice in the matter (although having the choice as a child wouldn't have been any better). I never had a chance to be outside of that boiling mess until I was old enough to distance myself on my own.

This story isn't just mine. Countless students in my classroom, in the halls of my school, in your classrooms, and in your schools deal with similar abuses. They aren't given choices. They aren't asked if they want adult stressors put on them before having to write an essay or take a standardized test or sit still during a school-wide assembly.

For some teachers, it's hard to imagine that such stress is pushing down on kids in middle school or high school, or even in elementary school. For other teachers, it's a harsh reality they have already experienced. It doesn't matter which group you fall into; what matters is that you're there every day for your students. Whenever my gut tightened and my head pounded because of issues at home, it helped to be at school. I felt better every time my teachers smiled at me. I felt better when I felt safe.

You might not always know about the troubles your students are facing at home. That's okay. You still can be intentional about the influence you have in their lives.

I grew up thinking my dad was the good guy. I idolized him. He was funny, strong, a talented drummer, and he had an infectious charm. But all of that was a cover-up for what he really was, what he really did to his children, and what he really did to his wife.

He convinced me that my mom was the sole drug addict between them and that he didn't know what was wrong with her. Reality and later confessions would reveal that he was feeding my mother his pills to keep her hooked on them and on him. He was feeding an addiction they both had. Part of it was her choice, without a doubt, but much of it was his doing, at least early on.

I would be so angry, confused, and frustrated when my mom would be out of her mind and drugged up. My dad and I would leave her in the house alone while he took me to baseball practice. I remember asking him what was wrong with her, why she was always "messed up."

He would answer, "I don't know, Jake."

If I could adequately describe the anger I feel as I recall that line, I would express it here, but I can't.

One by one, as I grew up, these lies collapsed in on themselves, as all lies inevitably do. No lie can stand under the weight of itself for too long, but this doesn't stop the liar from clinging to it. Anyone who has ever lived with addicts knows what I'm talking about. It's infuriating to watch, and once you get past the anger, it's simply sad.

The only thing addicts love more than their addictions is their lies. Maybe it's because they hate what they've become and it's easier to craft a story than it is to live their own lives, or maybe it's because lies are the best enablers. I don't know. They cling to them, though. They mold them. They bathe themselves in them until there is no discernible difference between the lie and the liar. That's their hope, at least, their desperation.

Family, friends, co-workers, and others are often able to see the addicts in their lives for what they are. If not immediately, then they realize it painfully over time, and when they do, things get really hard. It's impossible for me to describe how many times I stared at my mom in complete defeat as she denied the various lies I caught her in. On a daily basis, I would break down the fragile façade of our lives, and my family would respond by frantically trying to restack the bricks. To this day, their hands are dusty and raw from it.

Addicts can't let go of their lies until they truly see what everyone else (who's sober) sees, but nothing can force them to see it, and we can't always stick around until they do.

At some point, the problems caused by addicts and abusers slowly morph into a burning building. As the place burns, innocent bystanders realize that they need to get out or they'll die among the flames.

Some people choose to burn. I didn't.

When I got older and could make decisions for myself, I began to distance myself from my family. I began to see that there was a world where constant anxiety, fighting, fear, and hate wasn't the norm, a world that wasn't built on a foundation of lies. I started to think, to hope, that perhaps the world held some truth in it, somewhere.

Not everyone gets to this point. Not every student tortured by a chaotic and abusive home life makes it far enough to see the other side of the divide between healthy and unhealthy. Some don't even reach the point where they can break the habits instilled in them by unhealthy influences.

I consider myself lucky because I had a small group of friends, aunts, uncles, and cousins who stepped in when they could. So many people encouraged my skills and desires. I am most grateful for the teachers and other educators who were always there and never let me down. They were in the classroom, supporting their students, supporting me, the best way they knew how, over and over again.

I'm thankful they fought for me even while they were having to deal with demanding jobs and managing their personal lives. They fought for every single one of us. We were more than scores or data. We were people.

In the end, I felt there was more. I *needed* there to be more, so I started to explore.

The first step to escaping the darkness is to find a light.

I was raised Southern Baptist, though it was what I would call a watered-down version of what people think of when they hear the name. Unlike many people who pull away from their child-hood faith in their teenage years, I didn't do so because of bad experiences in the church. I pulled away because of its connection to my family. It wasn't a conscious decision, but in hindsight it's obvious that in my escape from the burning building I was drop-ping one thing after another to run faster and farther away from the wreckage of my family. My faith fell away just like my admira-tion for my father.

Free from any beliefs whatsoever, I roamed the bookshelves of my high school's library, looking for any ounce of truth I could find. I loved books growing up, so it seemed like a logical place to start.

I probably read more books my freshman year than I did in all of my years growing up. I consumed them religiously—Bradbury and Melville, Rowling and Rothfuss. I read Hawking and Dawkins and Hitchens and Darwin and Lewis and Jung and Freud. I read. I learned. I experimented with big ideas and controversial ideas and random philosophy books I can't remember (I'm pretty sure I read a whole book about the concept of infinity, even though math was the bane of my existence), and all of that was just in the first semester of my freshman year. I would go on to read more and more until I formed new almost-beliefs about the world. I say *almost-beliefs* here because I was very much against the idea of locking myself into anything. Any form of dogma was a sickness to me. My father believed in dogma. His house rules were dogma. He was dogma. I didn't want any part of it.

My searching led me to a confrontational empiricism. As far as I was concerned, if it couldn't be replicated in a lab or proven with hard science, it wasn't worth considering. And boy, did I let people know. I argued—vehemently, compulsively—with anyone who would listen.

I am thankful my beliefs have evolved since then. I no longer subscribe to such dangerous reductionist ideology, nor do I think everything worth exploring needs to be lab-testable. Why limit our understanding to the technology of the time? Even though I've grown from where I was, however, it would be wrong to suggest that this phase of my life wasn't instrumental in shaping the person I would eventually become.

Thanks to some amazing teachers who cared about me, inspired me, and let me be the angsty asshole I was, I developed some useful skills while shaping my initial empiricist worldview. A love for evidence and logic, the ability to reason through complex ideas without jumping to overreaching conclusions, and the skill and respect for reasonable debate have all contributed so much to my life. It was in honing those very skills that I was able to determine what I wanted most in life—purpose.

I believe helping their students find purpose should be the goal of every educator.

— Lesson 3 —

You Have a Purpose

believe most people become teachers because they want a job with purpose. The minds of the young and the drive to make a mark on this earth are a perfect combination for achieving just that. People become teachers because they want to be a part of something bigger. On some level they realize helping others is the key to making a difference, to having a purpose.

It's a good thing this is what's driving most of us, because our students demand this from us every second of every day. From the moment they take their seats on the first day of school, they demand that we live with purpose. When that student is up, wandering around for the fifth time that day, they demand that we remember our purpose. When they are defeated, confused, lost, sad, angry, tired, or disrespectful, they demand, demand, demand that we remain committed to our purpose.

No one ever said teaching was easy. It's not. Having someone demand that you do something is never easy. It's exhausting, no matter who you are. Eight percent of teachers leave the profession annually, a turnover rate that offers a glimpse into how taxing the job of teaching is. Tens of thousands of educators decide early in their career that the pressures of the job are just too much to handle.

When we are aligned with our purpose, however, the intense demands of our students and the sheer importance of our work fuel our efforts in the classroom. We see the needs of our students—the massive, overwhelming need they have to be loved, understood, and encouraged—and we work until we feel like we can't push anymore, and then we push again. The truth is, and you're already saying it to yourself, we rarely feel like those needs are fully met or that our work is done.

So we keep going.

Many of us burn out.

I believe some teachers leave the profession because they got into it for the wrong reasons. This isn't a bad thing, mind you, just an observation. I don't believe liking kids is enough to drive the work you must do day in and day out. You must like the kids *and* dealing with their parents. You must like the kids *and* handling all their drama. You must like the kids *and* the process of teaching them respect, even when it appears they will never understand the concept. You must like the kids *and* fighting for their right to a proper education, even when every new district, state, or federal policy seems to be contrary to that goal. You must like the kids *and* teaching them the manners they should have learned five years ago or even five minutes ago when you gave the instructions. You must like the kids *and* the grind of lesson planning, assessment creation, and data analysis, because you know it all leads back to the important work we have to do: helping kids find their purpose. You must love the kids, and you must love the job.

Loving what you do does not mean there are parts of the job that don't need to change. On the contrary, I believe we should do away entirely with data for data's sake, seeing kids as nothing more than a number to be counted, and our reliance on terrible programs we force our most at-risk kids to interact with. But we should love the work of discussing these broken pieces. We should use the challenges of our profession to help guide us away from destructive practices and into more student-focused and humane policies.

The men and women who get into teaching simply because they like kids—and not because they truly and deeply love the wrenching, endless, elbow-deep work it takes to guide children through the public-school system—will burn out and leave.

It's okay to be honest about this trend. Teaching has long been a profession people play up in their heads as something it isn't. We can romanticize what we do, viewing it as some Robin Williams film. I'm guilty of this too, but the truth of the matter will always be that what we do is work. Teaching is a job, and it needs to be done with passion, hope, and perseverance. To change what's wrong with it, we must love it. When teachers get into the classroom they must be ready to do *the work*. Some realize they're not ready or willing to do that work, and it's okay. There's no shame in leaving if you find out teaching isn't what you thought it would be.

But what about the other teachers who leave? The veterans who have lived in the classroom for much of their adult lives. The superheroes who inspire young minds, teens, and the middles each and every year. Why do they leave?

As of writing this book, I'm in my fourth year of teaching and my third year of teaching sixth-grade English Language Arts. Thanks to a summertime visit to The Ron Clark Academy in

Atlanta, Georgia, a campus designed as a model for some of the most innovative teaching in the world, this school year started off with more energy, creativity, and resolve than any of my previous years. I was on a massive high after meeting all those RCA teachers, listening to their philosophies on education, and discussing what it is and what it should be. Seeing students and teachers walk on desks—a subtle sign that the work we do doesn't own who we are—hearing music thump from room to room, often with actual drums and guitars, and witnessing chants, call-backs, and deep, beautiful teaching take place is a revolution to an educator who has never seen the RCA teachers at work. It was like being baptized. I walked out of the academy feeling "born again" as a teacher, and I was ready to take on the world.

After our school's first few getting-to-know-you days, I was finally with my students in my classroom, which was newly redesigned and Ron-Clarked with the help of my wife. I was wearing a suit and tie and giving my all to my bright-eyed sixth-graders. I remember being struck by how joyful they were. Joy was there on their faces when they walked in and saw all the lights around the classroom. Joy was there when they saw me stand on a table for the first time (the only exception being one girl who was extremely concerned I was going to die and promptly asked if my boss knew what I was doing).

In those early moments, I was able to capture them, inspire their curiosity, and increase their drive to come to school. Yes, kids wanting to come to school. What an idea, right? I worked hard to plan those early moments for my students, channeling as best I could the feeling I experienced at RCA. I wanted them to know that Mr. Chastain's class was going to be an experience, not just another hour out of their lives where they were forced to sit under fluorescent lighting and work on anything but what they actually wanted to. By exhibiting energy and fun, I set the groundwork for being able to teach them discipline. By being bigger and louder than they expected, I piqued a curiosity I could later harness to rigorously explore multiple genres of literature. By showing them my commitment, I garnered a basic respect that would help smooth the way when I redirected their actions later on.

That is the job. It's all wrapped up in those moments. The good and the bad. The inspiring and the defeating. Capturing kids' hearts, minds, and souls.

I love being able to inspire my students to question and to laugh, but pushing them is work. It's not always easy to coax middle schoolers out of their intellectual comfort zones, and you have to make sure you're there for them when they fail. That part, however, is what most teachers cherish. It's what makes many educators—those who truly love cultivating young minds—stay for so long.

It's all the other parts of the job—to-do lists sent via email, school-wide initiatives rolled out with little or no explanation, meetings and more meetings—that push the new and veteran superheroes to leave earlier than planned. These burdensome pieces clog the machine and do very little to help teachers develop their passions and talents. They drag us so far away from our purpose that we give up altogether and quit. Sometimes they compel us to quit even though we still remember our purpose, making it all the more painful.

When a complaint or concern is brought up about a change in policy, procedure, or curriculum, the quick response it that teaching is about the kids and not the teacher. While this sentiment is true on many levels, this kind of reaction to teacher concerns is also a massive part of the problem in education. We as American society do not respect teachers enough, which is why we don't pay them a reasonable, professional wage. It's why teachers have to form Facebook groups to lobby or block-vote for politicians who are pro-education and why we have teachers leaving the profession left and right.

I'm sure most of the people who repeat this sentiment—that teaching is about the kids and not the teacher—mean well, but I doubt they have considered the repercussions of such a one-sided belief. Many haven't bothered to ask what effects this line of thinking is having on our teachers.

If teaching is about anything, it's about relationships. Teachers must have relationships with each other, administration, parents, and students. Our lives get exponentially more difficult if any of those relationships are out of balance (and they often are). Relationships that are one-sided are doomed to fail. When we say, "Teaching is about the kids and not the teacher," we are setting up our relationship with teachers for failure.

How can we look at our teachers—seriously taking into account the stress that accompanies working with young minds every day—and say, "You don't matter. Your happiness isn't important"?

I'm sorry, but if you truly believe the joy and happiness of our educators is secondary to anything happening in the classroom, you are part of the problem that is driving our passionate educators away.

A teacher is there to inspire learning in students. A teacher is there to facilitate, guide, and correct. A teacher is there to support kids when they need it, when they ask for it, and when they absolutely believe they need no help from anyone. A teacher is there to love a kid when that same kid is being disrespectful, or even violent, and when that kid comes to school hungry because their parent, for whatever reason, didn't feed them breakfast. A teacher is there to teach all the official and unofficial standards as well as basic manners, school etiquette, and common sense behaviors— how to raise your hand, how to be patient, how to disagree with someone, how to settle an argument, how to put on deodorant, how to be kind, how to stand up for someone, how to find a great book, how to take care of property, how to accept discipline, how to voice a complaint, how to wash your hands, and how to do any number of things that come up in a classroom over the years. It's unpredictable at times and yet totally and completely a part of what it means to teach pre-K through twelfth grade in today's schools.

Our educational institutions cannot continue do any of that successfully if they always treat the teacher as the least important piece of the puzzle.

If teaching is about the kids, and it is, then it must also be about the teacher. Administrators and coaches: if you're reading this, I'm asking you to seriously look at your educators and appreciate them for who they are and what they need. Listen to them. Stop seeing their needs and wants as secondary. If they are in their position for the right reasons, and most are, then they aren't complaining because they are lazy. They aren't resisting change because they are jaded. They are fighting for what they believe is best for their students. And I'm sorry to say this, but you can't say, "Teaching is about the kids, not the teacher," and in the next breath say, "Now we want you to do this thing that does nothing for students but makes our management job easier."

If teaching is truly about the kids, if you truly believe that, then let teachers be driven by their purpose, as long as that purpose is in line with serving the groups of kids before them. Don't squash it with whatever you think is more important. A teacher is just as important and essential as the students and their learning. You cannot have any of these pieces in isolation. Classrooms are delicate ecosystems. The moment you start poaching any piece of it, you bring it closer to possibly falling apart and failing.

All of you teachers who have ever felt like you wanted to quit or questioned if you should still be teaching or whether it's still worth it, ask yourself the following questions:

Are you living purposefully in the classroom?

Are you fighting for your students?

Are your decisions driven by data, emotion, or both?

Are you deciding to do what's easy or what needs to be done for your students?

Are you going through the motions because your plate is full, or because you've lost focus?

Are you supporting your students the way you know they need to be supported, or are you just following initiatives?

Are you in alignment with your "Why"?

Are you supported by your team and your administration?

Are you asking for help?

My fourth year of teaching has been better than any year before. And yet, I can't help but realize that, even with extreme love and commitment to my classroom, I'm still having to fight doubts. I'm still having to fight for the fact that I, the educator in my classroom, matter. My happiness is not secondary, but primary, and in conjunction with the students, their learning, their safety, and their care.

I have a purpose.

We have a purpose.

And quite frankly, there is a job to do.

— Lesson 4 —

Embrace Firsts

I don't know about you (and I say this with laughter), but I was a terrible teacher my first year. I loved the kids, the job, and my coworkers, but I was not good at it. Not even close. Those who saw that version of me are nodding their heads as they read this.

I didn't go to school to teach. My first degree is in communications, because I thought I wanted to go into business and marketing to use my love for writing and creating in an industry that paid decently. I quickly found out that business bored me. It was more about numbers and board meetings than I cared for, and I quickly changed paths and worked to pursue a career in education.

As fate would have it, I was still in contact with my high school teacher and mentor, Mrs. Hammer. She was generous—and brave—enough to set up an interview for me at the middle school where she worked. I interviewed for an education aid position and ended up walking away with an offer to teach U.S. History on a probationary certificate through an alternative certification organization.

If you find this surprising, imagine how I felt! Events like this one, where I fall into a circumstance that blooms into something magnificent, have formed major pieces of my life. I can't explain how they happen; they just do. I'm fully aware of how crazy they are, and I'm thankful for each and every one of them.

My experience in the classroom was absolutely zero on day one. I hadn't even taken a substitute position to get my feet wet. I was as green as they come.

I had passion, though, and a deep, driving purpose. My previous job had left me feeling dead inside and had given me a renewed desire to make my life meaningful. It was a brief taste of an adult life with a meaningless, soul-sucking job, and I wanted no part of it. This realization allowed me to refocus on what truly mattered to me.

The kids saw this and fed off of it, to an extent. I wasn't the best at lesson designing or classroom management, and I wasn't good at responding to student needs in the best way, often yelling, which is rarely, if ever, a good call. I had a desire, however, to get better. I wanted to live up to the high expectations my own teachers had set. I wanted to actualize the purpose I'd found in teaching.

I'm always jealous of new teachers who rock out their first years. Some people, many of whom I've had the pleasure of working with, come in and are immediately rock stars in the classroom. Me? I was, on many occasions, the part of the movie where the substitute is being overtaken by a class full of teenagers, except I was the full-time teacher. My poor, poor teaching partner in the portable with me had to listen to the chaos of my classes all year.

Let's take a moment of silence for all of the partners who've taken care of us first-year teachers.

Cue head nod.

In all seriousness, I can't stress enough how awful that first year was. So much went wrong. I have vivid memories of my first official observation by my principal, who watched my classroom all but burn down as I tried to run an interactive lesson. I had no control. Students wandered around to different groups when they should have been working. Some asked questions they should have known the answers to, while others simply played, clearly off task and talking way too loudly. All the while, my principal took her notes and probably tried to look for the silver lining as she wondered if she'd made a mistake in hiring me.

Maybe you've had a similar experience. If not, I applaud your ability to be a rock star.

After that observation, I wasn't sure what would come next. I knew it didn't go well. I knew I wouldn't get high scores on any part of my evaluation. I felt a pressure to perform better because of how much of a risk the school took on hiring me the way it did, but I also knew my principal and was confident she would guide my development in ways I needed.

In one of our many talks, she told me it was my ability to reflect on my work that made me a teacher who could be successful. I took it as a small compliment that first year, but over the course of the years that followed, I came to realize that the truth of her statement applies to all of us. Reflection is essential to bring about meaningful change.

Teachers must be able to look at their work and judge it. Emotion has to take a back seat. It isn't about feelings at this stage of our work. We have to improve quickly and willingly. I don't know if I would have made it my first year if I hadn't been willing to accept critical feedback from all of the great teachers and coaches around me. It's possible I would have made it another year without change or improvement, but eventually I would have crumbled under the weight of my mistakes.

I am thankful I was able to adapt. I learned to embrace the fear and struggle of firsts.

No one can tell you how your first year of teaching will go. You have to figure it out and show up every day. No one can tell you how it feels to get the results back from that first test. You have to stand there and face it, whatever the numbers say. No one can tell you how to regain control of a class after it's devolved into chaos. You have to slog it out in the trenches.

Preparation is important, but the job of teaching also requires being able to adapt. So much of what we do has to be learned as we do it and then reflected on later for improvement. That requires honesty. I've seen many teachers delude themselves into thinking they're doing great work in the classroom when they're not. They hide behind their desire to be great, instead of desiring to get better, and students pay the price. They make excuses for their students' low performance, even blaming the students directly instead of reflecting on lesson design and classroom management. They pat themselves on the back for a project they created instead of seeking advice from more experienced educators about how they might have elevated the assignment.

No one wins when teachers lie to themselves.

We need to be honest about what's going wrong, but we should also be honest about the great stuff. My first year, in terms of focus and control, was trash, but there was some true magic sprinkled in there as well. I got to experience my first lesson where kids were engaged. I got to see my students light up with excitement as a piece of history finally fell into place and clicked. I got to experience what it was like to care about my students so much that I looked forward to hearing about their daily lives and being an ear for them when they needed it. I got to learn and get better at an amazing job.

In a wonderful example, the next time I was observed that first year, I planned a huge lesson for my Pre-AP U.S. History class with the help of my academic coach and good friend. It was called "Stump the Expert," and it allowed a student who was doing great in class to serve as an expert on a particular topic. After a period of time for both the expert and the class to research and learn, the students would write questions to try to stump the expert. Standing in front of the class, the expert would read the questions and answer them on the spot without seeing them in advance. If the expert survived the task, they got to sign their name on a big chart in the room and were given prizes and plenty of praise.

During the lesson, I hyped up the room by playing the Chicago Bulls theme song. The students were jazzed. The atmosphere was buzzing with excitement and tension. I'm pretty sure I giggled at least once.

Would someone be able to stump the expert and bring glory to the class? Or was the expert so knowledgeable that they would reign supreme?

Question One came and was answered with ease. Piece of cake.

Question Two was much of the same, and then they got harder and more advanced. Before my principal or I knew it, we were watching students fling high-level questions they had come up with themselves at this student who had taken time to educate himself. On all fronts, it was student-driven MAGIC.

Then the music was slowly turned down.

The final question was asked and answered—correctly!

BOOM!

No one could stump the expert! My first-ever mega lesson was done, and students were amazed at the intelligence of the expert in the room. He was praised, students were engaged, and guess who got to guide the lesson review when we looked back on this standard? The expert!

There were things wrong with the lesson. There were pieces I would have changed in hindsight, but it was my first great lesson.

◇◇◇

Reflecting on the successes of our teaching days is just as important as learning from the bad. We can easily create a destructive mental environment for ourselves if we don't see the good in what we've done, if we don't look at the magic that happens even when our classes aren't the best.

The good we find will drive us when we are down. It will keep us alive when we feel like we're dead on our feet. We must stay inspired, so inspired that even when a lesson collapses or a student hates our work, we are more creative and driven in our solutions than ever before.

Some people feel like praising themselves isn't being humble and that it's a cocky thing to do. There's truth to this, but this mindset can also be toxic if taken to the extreme. We need praise just as much as we need criticism. We will never get better if all we do is beat ourselves down. It's okay to know you did something well, and it's okay to feel proud, just as long as you are looking at it all with correct perspective. We have to constantly check the lens we are using.

I love looking back at my first year and seeing the good in hindsight. How amazing is it that, though I wasn't a skilled teacher, I still have moments I'm able to be proud of? I didn't have the best scores or the best behavior or the coolest lessons, but I had some of each at different times because I was willing to improve.

I was able to have some great firsts during my first year.

I love embracing firsts, because it's the only way we will ever get to seconds and thirds.

As my year went on, I tried a bunch of things. I co-taught with an amazing partner who taught me as much about life as she did about handling a class. I pushed myself to understand kids who made me want to pull my hair out.

Most importantly, I began learning how to love, quite literally, for the first time.

The life I had growing up injected a darkness into my soul that I carried for a long time. It's still with me, but its power and reach have diminished over the past four years. Seeing those kids and working with them day in and day out released me from my mental cage. The cynicism that had become so pervasive in my thoughts and beliefs began to die when I realized how amazing those kids were.

On some level, I think I knew this before I saw the kids in my classroom. Coming face to face with my students' intricate thoughts, hopes, and dreams uncovered the light in my own soul, the light that had been lying there under all the darkness all those years.

— Lesson 5 —

Take Care of Others

We never shied away from loud music in my house. Walking in at any given moment during the night or day, you would hear my father playing Metallica's *Black Album* or Rush's *2112*. If my mom was running the show, you might hear Melissa Etheridge or Shania Twain. My sister would be jamming to Backstreet Boys or Eminem, while I would be playing any assortment of music, including Korn, Bon Jovi, or AC/DC. My brother liked music too, but he was content to have his headphones on and stay in his private world.

In any case, music filled my home almost as much as yelling did. During the summer our lives featured many different soundtracks, often playing at once. My mom would blast her music in the living room while my sister and I dueled on opposite sides of the wall with our own tunes.

For me, the wall of sound was protection. I'd set up my stereo with a mixed CD of my favorite songs, sit on my bed, and shake my head for hours at a time. With my eyes closed, nothing could hurt me, and nothing existed except me and the music.

Shaking my head might sound odd, but it was an early coping mechanism I developed. It was a form of meditation, to a degree. If music was playing and I was alone, I would shake my head back and forth along a latitude. I'd done it since I was a very young child, and it stayed with me until my teens. Today, if I'm really sick, I still have the desire to sit up and shake my head.

One day I was in my room, zoned out and shaking my head back and forth, and my mom came in. She said *we* had a family announcement. I didn't know who she meant by *we,* but I got up, paused my music, and walked into the living room.

My father was sitting in his favorite spot on the couch, giant mug next to him. He was watching some fishing show, and I knew something was off because of the face he was making. It was kind of an amused face, without the signs of laughter—a little like a sick clown. It was a face I knew well. The face of change.

My sister came in the room and blurted out, "I'm pregnant!"

She was smiling nervously, but she seemed genuinely excited. Not sure how to react, my mom eyed my father for direction, but the puppet master was looking off into the distance, an eyebrow slightly raised.

I was too young to get the significance of what was happening, so the facts didn't hit me as hard. I wasn't sure if I should be excited or not, and I listened to the entire discussion with a kind of quiet indifference. They started talking about logistics, such as who the father was and if she would stay in school. I think the plan was that she would try to stay in school, but maybe they already knew they would try to homeschool her, given that she was only fifteen with a baby on the way.

My nephew was born when I was eleven, and the family focus centered on him. If there were any arguments or fights over the fact that my sister had become a teenage mom, I don't remember them. We all simply accepted this as our new life and continued on.

Having a baby in the house changed a lot. It changed me.

Just being around him, holding him and learning to take care of him, opened my young mind to innocence. All my life I had known pain and suffering I could do nothing about, and suddenly there was this baby who needed me. It was as if I subconsciously realized we were all born innocent, and I wanted to preserve that innocence at all costs.

I became protective of my nephew, seeing myself in him as I looked at this child who had been born into a family with countless problems.

He learned about those problems far too soon, even before he could walk.

◇◇◇

My sister was out, and my mom was taking care of my nephew. It was late, and he'd woken up a few times already, but it seemed like he was finally out for the night as the hours passed without a cry.

Hope for a quiet night vanished as he cried out again, wanting relief from the pain his new teeth were causing him. I was in the living room, watching a movie and waiting for my mom to go to him. When she didn't, I made my way down the hall to wake her.

She was slow coming to—even with his cries from across the hall—and I had to shake her to get her to focus.

My gut was already tightening at the sight of her glazed look. *Maybe she wasn't messed up. Perhaps she was still just half asleep.*

She finally made it out of bed, walked groggily to my sister's room where the crib was, and got my nephew out to try to calm him down. I watched for a moment out of instinct and concern for my nephew, but when she seemed to have it under control, I left her alone and went back to the living room.

Minutes later, I saw my mom walking down the hall to the bathroom. *He probably had a wet diaper.* I continued watching my movie until I realized they hadn't come out of the bathroom in a while. I turned the television down and listened.

Silence.

My stomach and heart started to pulse again in unison. I stood up and made my way to the bathroom. The door was cracked and the light was on, but I couldn't see anything from where I was standing, so I pushed it farther open.

My mom was on her knees, slouched over and asleep—or rather, in a pill daze. My nephew was on the floor, his dirty diaper half open. She'd passed out while changing him.

A flash of anger coursed through me and my breath came up short, but I controlled it and crouched down.

"Mom," I said as sternly as I could.

She didn't rouse.

"MOM!" I yelled, shoving at her shoulder a little.

Her eyes shot wide and then lidded over as she looked around. "WhatI'mdoingit," she mumbled in a monotone voice. No inflection. "I'm doing it . . ."

I watched as she reached for the baby, who seemed content to be out of his crib and in the bright restroom, and struggled to lift him.

"Mom!"

She arranged him to try to take off the diaper, but her hands and fingers were clumsy. It was like watching an ape try to use a phone.

"Mom!"

Managing to unfasten the diaper, she lifted him up with two hands to remove it and promptly lost her balance. Tumbling forward, she whacked the baby's head against the bathroom floor.

"MOM!" I yelled, knocking her out of the way and taking charge of the diaper change. "You're messed up. Get out, you're messed up!"

"I am not!" she yelled back, a hand lazily swinging out at me. "I'm just tired, just tired."

I finished my nephew's diaper, put his clothes back on, and picked him up.

"Go to bed," I told her, shushing him as we walked down the hall.

In my sister's bedroom, I rocked him until he fell asleep, and then a little longer after he started dreaming. I stayed in that dark room, thinking and breathing and calming down. So many thoughts swirled in my head. *Where is my sister? Probably out again, as usual. Why couldn't my mom just stay sober? She must have timed it to get high and then pass out after he was asleep. Should I wake my dad, or should I just handle everything myself? I know how to change diapers and make formula bottles. I don't need my mom or dad to help. I wonder . . .*

After a while, I laid my nephew back in his crib and left the room. It was the dead of night, and this was my life.

I walked down the hall to the bathroom and found my mom where I'd left her on the floor. The anger had given way to a weary anxiety, and I went through the usual routine: I got her a cup of water, walked her to her room, and got her into bed beside my dad.

On my way back to the living room, I made sure to grab a Coke so I could stay up and take care of the baby if he woke up. When the movie ended, I started another, watching until light began to shine in through the windows and my father got up and told me to go to bed.

◇◇◇

I hate telling these stories. It's hard to believe they belong to me at all. My life has changed so much since those years; it's as if I'm looking at an alternate timeline of a life that almost happened.

The reality is that this did happen, and it changed me. Most of all, it gave me a sense of justice. It wasn't something I could clearly articulate at that young age, but I sensed when things were wrong and needed to be put right. I sensed how awful the world can be to those who deserve it the least—children and the powerless—and that I needed to do something about it when I saw it.

It's unjust when an adult's negligence and indifference lead to the suffering of children and the powerless, and it's even more appalling when an adult actively causes that suffering. My father held the power in our family so that no one else had any, and my mom allowed her pain to manifest in destructive ways. Living inside that storm, I could only do so much, but I stood up and helped when I could.

In a world where suffering is so pervasive, deciding to act is making a choice to resist complacency and empower the human spirit. It's easy to get overwhelmed by the suffering we experience. It eats us up and drains us of the energy to move and think. For many years my own suffering built up in my system, producing an untamed rage towards the world.

The only antidote was taking care of others—reaching out and caring for my nephew, making sure my addicted mom made it to bed when she was high, and trying to stop my father from killing my mom when he beat her.

The antidote to anger, suffering, and the boulder of pain that weighs us down is taking care of others. The antidote to suffering is action.

When I feel the weight of the world or when my walls crash around me, I take action. I get up and do something. Sometimes it's as simple as cleaning the house, thereby taking care of my family, and sometimes it's recording a podcast to support thousands of educators. But it is always something for others.

I stumbled across this truth as a child, and it has served me well as I've aged.

Even in the darkest nights of the soul, one can act and bring some light back into the world.

Teaching, at its core, is an act against suffering. It is a stance we take against the injustice and ignorance of the world in the hope that we can create a better world. The care teachers take with their kids and the many ways they offer so much of themselves to their students are a testament to this claim.

Teaching is one of the greatest examples of a career in which we thrive when we support better, care more, and base our decisions on empathy. Teaching is an act against the fear, anger, and hate in the world. It is a light amidst the darkness.

It was a little surprising to realize the domestic violence and drug abuse I witnessed as a child had compelled me to embrace a life of compassion for others, but I'll never turn away from it. By living a life in which I constantly think about taking care of others, I have filled my mind and my soul with a positivity I wish I could shout through these pages to you so you could feel the same way.

The act of teaching matters. Taking care of others matters.

— Lesson 6 —

Be the Camera in the Room

I can't remember a time when fear wasn't a part of my daily life. If I try to think of a time when it wasn't, my mind might land on a happy memory of a party, playing the drums, or waking up on Christmas morning. But even those happy memories, deep within, have an underlying white noise of fear and anger. Parties were usually combined with arguments. When I was playing the drums, it was usually a reaction to what was happening in the house. And Christmas morning . . .

I'm not sure how old I was—probably around eleven or twelve, possibly younger. My father had given my mom a new video camera a day early so we could record the festivities.

This camera, while exciting to have, is probably the reason I have so many negative feelings associated with Christmas. Because of it, I was able to watch and re-watch the nasty bits of my family, the stuff a child raised in abuse learns to block out. It didn't help that I had a small infatuation with the device. For its time, it was a top-of-the-line camera. It had a fade out button, live effects, and a whole mess of settings.

I often remember events as being positive until something shows me otherwise. I used to remember that Christmas morning as being one of the best, but when I watched the video later on, the truth was plain to see: Mom slurring her words; Dad shoving his nagging, jagged, needle-like comments into his family's skin for no real reason other than to show some sort of barbaric dominance; the rest of us on edge but smiling all the while.

In that particular video, I was sitting cross-legged on our couch and my sister was recording. My hair was a mess, and I was wearing a T-shirt and basketball shorts. It was early but not too early. Despite being up for several hours, my brother, sister, and I had to wait for my mom and dad to get up, make their coffee, and hand out the Christmas gifts.

My dad was sitting in his usual spot, in his usual pajamas, with his usual cup. The small amount of hair on his head was wild, like mine. His mustache was thick and graying slightly. With his legs propped up and the recliner extended, he sipped out of his massive cup filled with light brown coffee. I can still smell it today as clearly as if I'm back in that room on Christmas morning.

My mom was on the floor in her pajamas, passing out presents. Our overweight Rottweiler was hanging out on the floor eating her new bone. My sister was talking about something to the right of me, and my older brother was slumped in the green recliner across the room, half asleep.

In my head, if I take a brief, casual stroll through this memory, I see it as a happy time. I was excited to be opening gifts. Dad was smiling, mom was laughing, and my sister and brother were doing their own thing, as teenagers usually do.

That camera, however, captured the truth—my mom's nervous and jittery behavior, my sister's voice a little too high and strained, my brother high or coming down from a high, and my dad wielding his words like weapons. The video took a leap, and all of our presents were opened, and my mom was asking us if we liked what we got. Although I had my obligatory stack of clothes, I was clearly more fascinated by the flashier CDs and video games.

The camera panned, and we were all smiling and laughing, and it was almost time to start breakfast. We all looked happy. I can't tell you what my family was thinking or what was going on behind the scenes—I was too young to really know then. I knew some of it—the mold that grew between the cracks in our family's façade—but not enough.

My mom got a piano that year, the kind with the keys that lit up so you could play along. The hit song on that piano was "My Heart Will Go On" from *Titanic*, and my mom would play it over and over again. She and my sister would take turns. It was Christmas night, and I was recording on the couch. I didn't see it then, and I don't remember it in my head this way, but whenever I see what the camera recorded, I see a mom who isn't sober. Maybe she's drinking, or maybe she's on her way down to a pill-induced low. It's not clear.

That scene, like so many of the happy memories I have of my family, was nothing more than a weak disguise. It was as if our joy was a thin layer of paint covering the rotting wood of our home.

At this point, I feel like it's important to say something very clearly: I don't look back at my life growing up and only remember the bad. The camera saw the bad, but my mind doesn't, not fully. My mind, despite knowing the truth of everything now, genuinely remembers these days as happy. My brain filters the scene and leaves only the stuff I enjoyed, for the most part. As a child it's hard to know you're unhappy when unhappiness is the norm.

Many people had it worse growing up than I did. My older brother did. He got it the worst out of anyone else in the family. He wasn't my dad's son, so my dad was meanest to him, calling him names like "sissy" for wanting to wear earrings and "wigger" for listening to rap and wearing clothes that were baggy. My brother was forced to do the brunt of the chores and was insulted when he did them wrong. He was abused more than all of us in the house, at least verbally. I consider his younger years worse than mine, but that's all I'll say about him. It's his story to tell.

As a teacher I have run into countless young people with homes that resemble what mine was. They come to school smiling and happy, play with their friends, high-five their teachers, and answer questions in class. But then they'll let something slip— mom is in jail, dad is in rehab, I'm living with grandma for a while, I hate my stepmom, my dad gets angry. Many kids bring these facts up bluntly in throwaway comments. It's as if they want to talk about the real problems around them, but they don't know how, so they just casually mention it in the hope that someone will hear it and help them. Perhaps some of these kids realize what their life is like and want out. Perhaps some are like I was and only *feel* the wrongness, never understanding until the scars are dark and deep.

In any case, I see kids in my classroom who remind me of what my life was like, and I see kids who have it worse. I don't know what it's like to be in foster care because your family is so strung out on drugs that you are taken away. I don't know what it's like to be beaten by your parents or stepparents. My dad never hit me, just chest pokes and threats and mental games. He saved the beating for everyone else. I don't know what it's like not to have food at home or electricity daily, but there were periods where I had no air conditioner in the middle of Texas summers and there was only ramen and frozen burritos to eat because my mom was in jail, money was scarce, and my dad was long gone. For many of our students, this is their reality every single day.

The tragedy and miracle of our jobs as educators is one and the same. We see how many of our students are suffering at home. We hear bits and pieces about the real-life issues they have to worry about at such a young age. We read their stories when they decide to share them. We see how they gravitate to dark novels at younger ages because that is the stuff they relate to. We see it, and we hurt for them. I get a stabbing sensation in my gut every time I see, hear, or learn about the awful world many of them live in.

It's not always readily apparent. They don't come in with signs hanging around their necks that say "ABUSED" or "HUNGRY" or "SCARED." Many of them act in such a way that you'd never guess the lives they live when they leave the school grounds. And then something happens, and reality hits you in the face.

The tragedy is seeing so much pain in our students.

The miracle is that we get to do something about it.

One strategy I have employed is working harder to create a safe community within my classroom. It occurred to me that I have the opportunity and the means to help my students build authentic relationships—with me, with each other, and with other people in their lives. I began to ask some basic but powerful questions: What if I shared a story about myself? What if I asked them to share one of their own? What if I sat down with a student in a moment of downtime and we just talked—teacher to student, adult to child, person to person? What if we had a pair-share about something happening in our lives? What if we did a team-building activity that was designed to foster community in our classroom?

I find more and more that if I create a place where students feel comfortable and are allowed and encouraged to use their voices daily, they begin to open up. We all have days when we feel like we're going through the motions. That's when making those connections is so vital. When I find myself feeling like nothing is truly happening in class, I turn whatever we are doing into a real experience that requires a human connection.

Sharing is powerful. It allows us to move closer to working out all kinds of fears and insecurities. Community is powerful, and there is power in letting our voices be heard.

We can't heal every child who comes to us broken any more than we can heal every broken piece of ourselves, but we can be the camera in the room. We can force ourselves to look more closely at our students, to see who they are and what they deal with, and to take action to be there for them.

If we open our lenses a little wider, if we zoom in just a little more, we can begin to see the sadness in their eyes. I was smiling as I opened those Christmas presents, but what was underneath that smile? I loved my new video games, but I would have been happy with nothing if it meant having a healthy home life.

During my years as a teacher, I have met so many students who get in trouble daily and who have a home life that is nothing short of tragic. It's such a cliché, but it's a cliché for a reason. If you don't know who these kids are, ask your administrators. They'll know because they're the educators who often deal with those kids the most. They seem to get into trouble at every turn. They destroy school property, insult teachers, and get constant zeros. They come off as more apathetic than you ever thought possible. I'm sure, by now, a few faces are appearing in your mind.

While not all of these students have rough homes, an overwhelming number of them do, and it kills me when I see these students being treated like second-class citizens by teachers or administrators. They celebrate when they're absent, gossip about them to other teachers, write them up quickly, yell at them early, and compliment them little.

I get it. We all understand why teachers and administrators vent and come to resent certain students. We've all probably done it.

But. We. Just. Can't.

We must be the miracle in those students' lives. I know they are frustrating, infuriating, and often the difference between a great day and a terrible one. They can make or break a lesson in seconds, but every student demonstrating an undesirable behavior is showing us a need.

A speaker at a Kagan training I attended shared a thought that I've remembered ever since: the key to helping our most frustrating students is changing our mindset. If we stop looking at that student who's destroying our lesson as the bane of our existence and instead as someone clearly demonstrating a need, we can flip our reaction to be more productive and healing for that young mind and ourselves. Sometimes a student is like a projector: if you're standing so that it's shining in your eyes, you're only going to see a blinding light; but if you move and look from a different angle, you'll be able to see the whole picture.

Students who come from homes like mine are not at fault for their upbringing. The way they act is a symptom of their abuse, fear, or loneliness. The students who struggle with self-control and behavior are the students who need us most. They need us to be constant and understanding. They need us to be compassionate even when compassion is the last emotion we want to embody.

When Jack acts out in my class, when he's being disruptive, rude, or apathetic, it's my job to breathe and watch, to see him and the truth he's trying to communicate. As the educator in the space, it's my job to realize that he's a real person in front of me with needs, dreams, and goals. He needs something from me in that moment. What he needs could be different from day to day, moment to moment, but the one constant is that he *needs*, and I must be there to give.

The students you are thinking about right now need you more than you could ever possibly know.

Trust me. I was one of them.

— Lesson 7 —

You Have a Choice

There were so many positives and negatives in my life. Many of them went hand in hand.

My love for music and ability to play it came from my need to escape my family when fights would break out. Music helped me when I needed to release built-up anger, much of which I didn't know how to articulate or even think about until later.

My desire to see the positive in negative situations came from years and years of dealing with dark nights where I would cry myself to sleep, only to wake up, go to school, and enjoy happier moments. Because school was a constant for me, I believe it trained my brain to always look forward to the positive, to the sun after the storm.

That willingness to push myself and keep going in adversity came from those long nights when I thought I would die or my mom would die or one of my siblings might die. I would push myself to stay up, stay focused, and try to help, even though I had no idea what I was doing.

My sense of purpose came from watching my family wallow in its own purposeless drama, anger, substance abuse, and self-pity for how their lives had turned out. I saw what that life looked like firsthand, and it instilled in me the idea that there must be purpose. It's not an option, not in my mind. Without purpose, life isn't life at all.

I could have kept up the family tradition of being addicted to anger, fighting, and drama, but I turned to music. I could have fallen into destructive behaviors without any plan for the future, but I chose action, mission, and vision. At the same time, I feel as though every one of these choices was made by accident or luck. I was just lucky enough to have good around me, and I gravitated towards it. I was lucky enough to go to schools that gave me experiences to look forward to. I was lucky enough to have teachers who cared and who were passionate about their jobs. I was lucky enough to be able to fit in, have friends, and have options beyond the circumstances I was born into.

One of the biggest concerns I have for the students in our hallways and classrooms who have home lives like mine is that many of them don't realize there is a choice at all. It terrifies and saddens me to know there are kids who have it worse than I did and have far fewer options of escape. It angers me to know these kids can go to school and not be lucky enough to be in a class where their teachers and fellow students love and respect them.

I had support in school, but many don't. It pains me to write it, but we have all seen, heard about, or worked with teachers who don't support all of their students in the most positive ways. These teachers are few and far between, thankfully, but even one is too many.

One teacher constantly yelling at students for not getting their work done, rather than trying to figure out the reasons why, is too many. One teacher ridiculing or belittling a struggling or misbehaving student, especially out of some misguided attempt at showing "tough love," is too many. One teacher failing to help a child find hope in the future is too many.

A great teacher can be the difference between a child making the choice for a positive life and making the choice to let themselves drown in their suffering. The more caring and compassionate teachers we put in front of children, the more likely they will be to believe they have a choice about how their lives will go.

Many students don't see their choices. They simply don't think about their lives in those terms. They just deal with the disappointments, fears, bad decisions, and consequences as they come. Untouched and unguided, they can end up on a massively destructive path. If they have guides along the way, however, teachers and adults who relentlessly engage, support, encourage, constructively discipline, empower, and love, they will have more reasons to act in positive ways.

Students who continuously hurt themselves and others do so for specific reasons, just like the students who continuously make positive and helpful decisions.

The fact that I was able to make several good decisions in my life, even though I lived in a destructive and, at times, hellish home, speaks volumes about the power of the other people in my life—my friends, their parents, and, most of all, my teachers.

My life is a testament to the will of those teachers, because while they were helping me make healthy choices, they were also juggling multiple classes and countless other students just like me!

Teachers decide what to do in class, what standards to hit that day, how to react to a student, when to help and when to let students figure things out on their own, when to change the course of a lesson, how to get students' attention, how to interpret data, when and how to assess, and the list goes on and on.

Some people thrive under the pressure of having that many choices to make every day. You see them in your department meetings or school gatherings. They're the ones who are always put together. They're having the time of their life because they enjoy the thrill of the job. It's like pressure fuels their very being.

Some are the exact opposite. They don't thrive under the pressure of having endless choices to make every day. Their personal lives get in the way. They want to focus on a few aspects of the day, and when all of the other stuff comes into play, they start shutting down or letting it affect the quality of their teaching.

Although I am speaking in generalities here, having both of these types of people is necessary in a school. Those who flourish when faced with many choices are often the best at making decisions quickly.

Can't decide what to focus on in a meeting?

Boom. They're there to help.

Can't decide which part of a standard or task to tackle first?

Boom. They've got it.

With that said, quick decision-makers can sometimes lack the nuance that educational decisions need. They often see the scope but not the depth. This is where the other type of person comes into play. That person is great at focusing on a few key things. They have the ability to take those quick decisions and add the depth needed to bring about true progress.

Both types of people can be obnoxious in their own right. Lateral decision-makers can be all over the place, moving from one thing to the next without slowing down to evaluate consequences and ripple effects. They decide, move on, and decide some more.

Vertical decision-makers can be too slow, taking too much time for discussion so that nothing really happens on a timely basis. They talk and analyze without ever solving the issue at hand or actually getting things done.

It's obvious that teachers can be any combination of the two types of people I've described here, mixing and matching strengths and weaknesses in a variety of ways.

Reflecting on my own tendencies, I can't help but be critical of the way I work. I tend to focus on the negatives of my work in my head and discuss the positives out loud. I'm not sure what that says about my personality, but the fact remains that it's how I usually function. The way I discuss my practices with people is on the positive side of the spectrum, while the internal dialogue I have with myself is predominately critical.

Combining that with the fact that I make a lot of lateral decisions and then later add vertical depth often leads me to an interesting product, though not always a product of the best quality.

Because I am one of those people who tends to like a lot of work and, by connection, likes having to make a lot of choices, I'm a lateral person by nature. I want to get it done when it needs to get done, whenever that is. Here's an example: I'll walk into my class with a heavy load of lesson plans. I know what I'm going to do. I have all of my boxes checked. Those choices were made laterally. I needed to figure out the week, and I did so, quickly. It isn't until I'm in the class, in the midst of a lesson, experiencing it with my students, that depth comes. I feel it out as I go. I see what needs to be extended and what doesn't. As the students show me their learning, their gaps, and their interest, I adjust the lesson and the week accordingly. My conferences in reading workshop become twenty-eight mini-lessons per class, all individualized for that student's needs in that particular time. It's as if I'm laying down railroad tracks as I'm riding the train. I know the destination, but I don't know the exact route we're taking to get there.

I love it.

I've talked to teachers who like having a system to everything they do. They fear the unknown when it comes to how a class will go. The stress of not knowing the specifics is far worse than being tied down to a lesson plan. Some go so far as to print out massive binders full of the year's notes, leaving little room for change as the school year goes on.

In the end, their results are more exact than mine. It's a strength to be so precise in their plans. It's a strength to be able to see so clearly what they want to do in their classroom. If this is you, be proud of it. Own it. If it brings positive results for your students and yourself, then it's what needs to happen in your space.

For one reason or another, I'm not very good at doing that. As with everything, this isn't constant. In some of the bigger lessons, I know exactly what will happen, but even those change as I work and make adjustments based on observation and student feedback. As an educator, it's me living in the moment.

Every teacher does this to some extent because it's impossible to plan for every possible outcome in a given day, but some, like myself, intentionally take this approach and thrive in it.

Maybe I'm biased, but I believe the power of choice is everything. I will always choose freedom over comfort. Unless it's necessary, I don't schedule anything. I feel like it ties me down. Why lock myself into something a week out when I might want to be doing something else? I want choice. I want to feel it in the moment, whatever it is.

Growing up, I didn't spend time wondering what to do with my life. I made choices quickly, saw what worked, and then deepened the choices that showed the most reward.

I chose to focus on writing as music revealed its limitations as a career.

I chose to focus on teaching when writing and then business revealed their limitations for my happiness.

I chose to focus on helping teachers across the world when it became apparent that teaching students, and thereby helping the world, required more than just managing my classroom.

I chose to focus on my own life when I realized nothing I could ever do or say would make a difference to my family. Nothing would keep my mom from popping pills, cheating on her significant others, or mistreating the people around her. Nothing would stop her from lying to everyone. It would have to be her choice.

Nothing I could ever do or say would make my dad into someone who didn't cheat, lie, and abuse those in his life. Nothing would help my father become something better.

I haven't spoken to my father in years, but I get wind of his actions from time to time. He makes an appearance here and there, like a recurring cold that's passed between family members. He shows up when my mom wants pills and he has some. He shows up at Christmas gatherings when he has nowhere else to go and my mom feels sorry for him. He goes to jail and gets out of jail. He shows up, and he infects. Always. This is his choice. He chose to control his family, to abuse them, to manipulate them, and now he chooses, by consequence, to reap what he sowed. I have no doubt his choices will eventually destroy him entirely.

Nothing I could ever do or say would make my sister be a good mom to her son and daughter. She chose to be the girl who got pregnant at fifteen, dropped out of high school, and now works odd jobs for days or weeks at a time before quitting for one reason or another. She chooses to use her own mental problems as crutches rather than actively trying to cope with them or get meaningful help, despite the help offered to her again and again. She chooses to let her kids suffer because of her actions, and she continues to suffer herself.

For years—*years*—I have wanted to help them. I tried to fix them. I wanted them to stop fighting all of the damn time, and more importantly, get off the drugs and finally get clean. But I've realized these things won't happen unless they make the choice to change.

I have come to understand that choices are powerful. Choices are everything, and until people choose to realize the destruction they create, until people realize the cost of eating the apple, they will never choose anything else.

I made a lot of lateral choices as I grew older. Nearly every one was a lateral move away from the craziness of my family. I didn't spend time wondering if I should move out of my house at eighteen; I just did it, in the middle of the night, as soon as I could. I didn't spend time wondering if I should go to college or what college I should go to; I just did it. I didn't spend time wondering if I should get a job or keep a job or pay my taxes or aim for promotions; I just did it.

I didn't spend time wondering if I should keep trying to be a part of my family; I just made the decision not to be. It was self-preservation. Many of my distant family members still choose to be a part of my immediate family's world. They condemn me because I don't. I'm the black sheep of the family because I escaped that world and built a family of my own. I understand where they're coming from, but they don't understand me. They didn't live the life I did. They weren't there for the constant fights or the fear I experienced every single day as a child. They didn't see me taking care of my nephew when his mother was gone and my mother was too high on pills to do it herself. They didn't see me screaming in my house, trying to control adults who had no control over themselves. They didn't see me pleading for my dad to stop beating my mom or for my mom to wake up while she was driving.

I had to make a choice and ask myself some tough questions. What would staying involved with that dysfunction do to the family I hoped to have one day? How would the drama surrounding their lives affect my own child? Would it seep into his mind? What would that do to him?

I knew the answer instinctively, and I chose accordingly. For the most part, I'm divorced from the family who raised me. I made a lateral choice to create a different life, and then I made vertical choices to deepen that life. I met my wife and deepened that relationship over years, almost a decade as of writing this. We created a life together.

Sometimes when I'm lying in bed with my wife, son, dog, and cat, I think about all the nights I spent crying in my room. I feel the love for my family, and I wonder how broken my parents must have been to have treated their kids the way they did and still do.

I feel sorry for them. I've seen their choices in retrospect and truly wish there were something I could do. I wish I could swoop in and show them that their lives are being wasted.

We live with our choices. They have made a vertical choice to continue living with pain, suffering, and endless drama.

I haven't.

— Lesson 8 —

Turn Your Negatives into Positives

I have no doubts at all that I have an inner desire for excess. Everyone in my family has the tendency, it seems. Gluttony is our curse. I'm not immune to it; I'm obsessive too.

It's like an itch. Something will happen or I'll see something, become infatuated with it, and obsess over it for days, weeks, or years—and I don't use the word *obsess* lightly.

Whereas my family has an obsession with being high, I have been able to channel my own obsessive tendencies into less destructive areas.

When I was in late middle school and early high school, I was deeply obsessed with music. The only thing I wanted to do was make it, play it, and record it. I played music with my cousin, who worked at a music studio, and we would spend hours and late nights just recording and creating. As far as I was concerned, it was all I wanted or needed. It consumed me.

That particular obsession eventually died down, though, and books took over. I wanted to read all of the best ones—and the weirdest ones—and be more knowledgeable than those around me. I read compulsively, buying them and borrowing them from the school library. For hours on end, I would sit in my room consuming page after page.

It turns out this obsession was closely linked to an obsession over identity. I began to question who I was and what it really means to be alive. I delved into religious ideology, adopting one idea for a few months, learning all I could about it, and then dropping it when the belief system didn't fulfill me.

I was obsessed with trying to become a successful fiction author for most of my early adult life. Though I still want to write fiction and give back to the community that gave me so much, I'm not compulsive about it anymore, not like I was a few years ago. While working at jobs I loathed, I became obsessed with the possibility of making it as an author because I wanted out of those jobs. I had started writing seriously a few years before this, but with the newfound inspiration to break away from the grind of bad jobs, I wrote furiously, finishing six novels in four years.

Today, I often get obsessed with forms of entertainment or thought, such as what I find in fantasy fiction. I love it—the worlds, the magic, the epic scale. I'll go through periods when fantasy fiction is all I'll read, and then I'm driven to play only fantasy games in which I can craft my own worlds. That usually keeps going and going until I burn out and move on to something new. I also go through cycles of non-fiction, following rabbit holes of ideas, or cycles of gaming, and even a little bit of self-improvement, if you can imagine that.

It happens with anything I'm interested in. The closer I am to it (i.e., something I create versus something I consume) the more intense my obsession becomes.

Along with the tendency to obsess comes the inability to have patience without conscious effort. I want everything at once. Maybe it's because I'm a millennial, but when I'm obsessed with something, when it's all I can think about, I'll try just about anything to get it as fast as possible.

Is this how my family feels with their drugs of choice?

Obsession, which can be called extreme focus if it's productive and positive, drives much of what I do. The speed at which I do whatever it is I'm doing, however, can also lead to negative consequences. Some things you just can't rush.

You can create a great lesson, but it takes time, distance, and different perspectives to truly see it from all angles. You can become a great teacher, but it takes practice, patience, and time.

I'm obsessive, and this can be my strength if I choose the right thing. I could have easily chosen to obsess over my problems, but I chose music. I could have chosen to obsess over my mom, dad, or family drama, but I chose books. I could have easily obsessed over any number of things, but I was lucky to have been given choices by my schools and the educators who worked there.

At this point in my life, work—teaching—is my obsession.

I've been criticized for my view on work by part of the network of teachers who follow the message I put out online. My view is that work should be a huge part of who you are, not just what you show up to do every day. If you choose the right work, it is as much a part of you as breathing.

I don't understand how people wouldn't want this. The thought of work as something separate, a place I am forced to be just to earn the money to pay bills until I can retire, leaves me cold. Why not live with your work? Why not do something that empowers your life instead of something that takes time away from it?

I've been told it isn't healthy to love work as much as I do. When I mention how I hate time off from work, some people scoff and tell me to get a hobby, hang out with my family (as if I don't), or simply relax and enjoy the time. Take a vacation, Chastain!

They mean well, and I get that, but not everyone understands what it's like to have a brain that obsesses. Many don't understand how serious I am when I say my work is literally a part of who I am.

I love my family, and I'm so grateful for the life I've built after so many years of pain and suffering; yet I still desire more. I want to *do* more.

It's not enough that I teach; I want to be the best teacher. It's not enough that I got one kid hooked on reading; I want them all to be hooked on reading. It's not enough that I do my job and go home; I want to continue improving at my job even when I'm away from school.

It's a compulsion. Maybe it's some residue of addictive personality that's in my genetic makeup or a lingering symptom of my childhood chaos, but I feel as if I have to keep *doing*. I'm not okay with just living my life and not having a greater purpose or an inner drive to gain more ground. I want to be a part of something that's bigger than I am. I want to make my mark and play my part. It's a desire I feel every morning when I wake up, every night when I go to sleep, and every time I waste a day doing nothing that furthers this goal.

If we want to make a difference, to truly make an impact on our students and their world, then we must let ourselves become the work. We must be consumed by it. The teachers making the biggest differences today do this. They are teachers to the core. It is who they are.

In a way, my deep obsession with work is my way of making up for lost time. My soul had so many holes that I was practically an afghan. As a kid, I never believed there was some greater purpose to my life. On all those long nights when I was struggling to stay awake to hear my nephew's cries or holed up in my room in fear as a family fight broke out, it never occurred to me that I might be in that situation for a reason. That's a hard thing to grasp when you're young. Hell, it's a hard thing to grasp when you're an adult.

Many people will say that my childhood unfolded the way it did so I could grow from it and have a desire to help others. When I reflect on many others who suffered just like I did and didn't make it out, I struggle to accept that it was part of a grand purpose or design. But I can't deny that the drugs and violence I lived with as a child transformed me as an adult and drove my focus to help others. I don't discount that in the least.

I'm grateful I made it out, that I had the choice to become obsessed with something greater than myself. I'm grateful one of the biggest criticisms people have of me is that I love to work at a job where it's my duty to help young people every single day.

Not everyone is as lucky, and not everyone has been fortunate enough to turn the negatives of their circumstances into positives.

Know When to Let Go

One day my dad came to me and asked if I wanted to play football. We were standing in the living room, and his eyes were twinkling with an idea he liked. I said yes, and later that day we were up at the rec center registering me for pee wee football.

I was large for my age, always the bigger kid. It wasn't until high school that I became average. As a child I was a little chubby, and I wasn't lanky, but I was tall. My wife just calls me a caveman, and in some ways, it's true.

Because of my size and my dad's willingness to lie about everything, he told the rec center I was older than I was. That meant I would be playing sports with kids who were a grade ahead of me. (At the time, I didn't know what he had done, but I did always find it strange that my sports friends were older than my school friends.)

After football, I was asked to play baseball. I loved baseball far more than football and jumped at the opportunity. My dad once again lied about my age, and again I was playing with kids who were older than me.

It was on this baseball team that I would meet some of my closest childhood friends. They would see the relative rise and fall of my family from the outside.

I had friends over to our house a lot. Sometimes they would stay for a day, and sometimes they'd stay for a weekend or an entire spring break. They seemed to like my house. Fighting happened less out in the open during those early years, and even when it did, my friends and I would be in my room playing games or outside throwing and hitting the baseball. Another thing my pals liked was that, unlike them, I was allowed to play all of the M-rated video games.

My home was the mecca of lack of supervision. As long as I was distracted, my parents were good to go, and so were me and my friends.

Some nights, though, the world I actually lived in—not the world outsiders saw or the one my friends thought was real—would show through. The truth of our home life would bubble to the top.

◇◇◇

It was a late weekend night. The air was warm, and the sounds of summer played melodies under the stars. My friend—we'll call him Landon—was over. I'd met him my first year in baseball, and we'd been on teams together ever since. He'd practically lived at our house since we met him. He would stay for days at a time, especially in the summer. He had become a part of the family.

We were hanging out with my sister at the behest of my buddy. I'm pretty sure he had a crush on her, so I tagged along with them while they drank and smoked cigarettes. I was still young enough that I didn't partake of either, although it wouldn't be much longer before I was given my first drink at thirteen.

The night wore on, and I realized my mom was getting more and more out of it. My father was out late—something he was doing more often—and my mom was left at home to brood.

Every once in a while, I'd get up from the carpeted garage where my sister, Landon, and I were chilling, and go check on her. Each time her words were getting more slurred. I checked her drink to determine if she was drunk or messed up on pills. Both, it turned out.

A while later, I heard her car keys rattle and rushed to check on her. Purse in hand, she was stomping out of the house in a crooked line.

"Where are you going?" I asked, my heart already thumping a little harder.

"I'm going to get your father," my mom snapped.

"Where is he?" I asked.

"Her house," she slurred back. She used the woman's name. I won't.

It was a summer night. I was dressed in a T-shirt and shorts, and the driveway's concrete was warm on my bare feet. Beads of sweat built up on my forehead.

"You're messed up," I said. A declaration.

"I'm not messed up, I'm pissed!" she answered.

"You're messed up! You can't drive," I insisted.

I tried to stop her, but she pulled away from me and got into our milk-chocolate Tahoe and slammed the door.

"Mom, you can't drive!"

I yelled this over and over through the glass, but it was like screaming at her from another world. I opened the door, and she yanked it back from my sweaty hands and locked it from the inside.

My heart slammed into my chest over and over again. I didn't want her to drive. She'd wreck and hurt herself or someone else.

I'd stopped her so many times before that I thought there was a chance she would listen, but her rage was powerful that night. It blinded her to the absolute terror and screams of her youngest son pleading with her just outside her car door.

I jumped on the side rail of the SUV and yelled louder through the glass, as if the volume of my voice mattered.

"Stop! You can't go!"

I was thinking she wouldn't drive away with me on it. She'd stop and turn off the engine.

A breath later, she started reversing the Tahoe to the street. She turned the wheel too soon and clipped over the edge of the curb. I heard her shift the transmission to drive, and then I felt the wind.

I screamed, my hands slick with sweat as I struggled to hold on. The streetlights flew past, and the neighbors' houses were dark and quiet. The peace of the dark street was a silence that seemed to suffocate my pleas for help.

As I held on, we bounced over the speed bumps of the street. I waited for her to slow down so I could get off, but she didn't. She just kept going faster until nothing existed but the sound of rushing air and the feeling of intense fear in my chest.

I convinced myself that we weren't going that fast. Irrational. My plan was to jump and run as soon as I touched the asphalt.

Another speed bump, and then I leaped. I tried to run, thinking I would be able to slow myself down, but a hot flash of pain seared my bare feet, and my knees buckled. I hit the street with a heavy thump, a noise my mother never heard.

The force was sudden, but the pain left quickly. Fear and adrenaline coursing through me, I limped to my neighbor's yard and then through the cool grass back to my house. The basketball goal in our driveway was like an obelisk in the desert. It wasn't in focus until I came close, and then I stopped and sat with my back against the solid metal pole.

My knees were bruised and bloody. The bottoms of my feet were scratched and bleeding. My breathing came in sharp stutters as my body began to react to what had just happened.

I sat and cried.

When I made it into the house, Landon and my sister were feeling good, their eyelids heavy. They asked where I'd been, and I told them I got thrown off the car trying to stop mom.

An awkward laugh was their only reaction, and I sat for a moment longer before heading to my room to play a video game.

A numbness replaced my pain as the hours wore on.

◇◇◇

Like so many of my memories, I've replayed this one endlessly in my mind. It's part of me. It changed me. That night taught me the power and danger of holding on.

The overarching theme of my family's tragic story is their inability to let go. They don't let go of their addictions. They don't let go of their need for pain. They don't let go of their constant fighting or incessant desire to lie to get what they want. They don't let go of their distorted view of the world.

I often wonder why I held on to that Tahoe for so long. In my head, I know I held on because I was scared and I wanted to stop my mom, but I can't help but wonder if there was something deeper happening. Perhaps a part of what makes my family the way they are also makes me the way I am.

You could say I held on because it seemed like the right thing to do. You could even say I kept holding on because I was too scared to do otherwise. Maybe you could say it was something more. Maybe I was just as addicted to the chaos as they were. I inherited the impulse to hold on, and because of that, I was dragged down the street by a mom who couldn't let go of her anger and didn't care whom she hurt in the process.

That impulse has led me to hold on to other things as well— good things, like my wife and son, my work, and my life.

To get to that point, to refocus and build a new life and a new purpose, I had to let go of my connection to my family.

As I got older and the stress became greater (because I actually knew what was happening and how damaging it was), I had to let go. It became clear to me that if I ever wanted out of the hell that world was and still is, I had to move on.

Since making that decision, I've been looked down upon by nearly every family member I have, but they don't understand what it was like to grow up the way I did. Even writing about my family in this book has left me with a tight chest and a few mild panic attacks in the night.

Sometimes letting go is all you can do.

We should believe people when they say that's their only option, because for many, it is.

As someone who's had to let go of so much, I know what I'm talking about when I say it's hard to do, and I succeeded and built a life I am proud of because I had some wonderful people surround me with alternatives, healthy and positive things to hold on to.

I grabbed on to school. Maybe not the actual school work, exactly, but the space and feeling of it. The friends, the activities, the teachers.

Sometimes the simplest things a teacher does are also the most powerful.

Classroom transformations, interactive lessons, and amazing experiences are worthwhile, and we should all strive to use these in our classrooms, but the most important thing is showing our students there is a better world out there.

If I hadn't had teachers who modeled and revealed this to me through quality relationships, I would have believed my family's reality was the only reality. I would have been caught holding on to the bombs as they continuously went off in my own home.

Just being there and showing students new and exciting things can make all the difference. By the time some of our students reach our classes, they have never seen an adult model happiness or honesty, so even the smallest gesture or kind word can make a profound difference. Being able to look at a child or a teenager when they're tardy, for example, and say, "I'm glad you're here today" instead of berating them for being late is powerful.

If we want our students to hold on to peace rather than violence, acceptance rather than rejection, effort rather than apathy, we must throw them the rope.

I held on to my mom's Tahoe because it was all I could hold on to. In that moment, it was all I had. A few moments later, all I had was pain.

There were more moments like that to come, but time passed, and eventually I had something else to hold on to—a future.

Take the Road Less Traveled

When I was in high school, I had some of the best teachers, but one stands out from the rest. She was my freshman English teacher, my senior English teacher, and went on to become a cherished mentor and friend.

Mrs. Hammer, with her bright insight, willingness to challenge me when I challenged her (or even when I didn't), and deep care for her craft, guided my thinking more than anyone I know. To this day I remember key conversations and discussions with her that not only opened my mind but also gave me the building blocks to do my own thinking and something else to hold on to when I needed it most.

One of the earliest memories I have of her is when I first walked into her room. There was a vibe that I, a freshman boy who was wearing a black Lamb of God T-shirt and in the process of growing out his hair, couldn't resist. She had "WELCOME TO HAMMER'S WORLD" projected on her screen. I was a lifelong fan before that first day was over.

I always looked forward to her class, and I don't remember one boring lesson. She engaged us at every turn, and not just with the lessons. She had great ideas and activities, but it was her verve and wit and passion that broke through our walls. She took our teenage angst and channeled it into an extreme positive energy, charming even the laziest among us. Her lessons always engaged us in interesting ways. She included small details that meant the world to me—touches of flair and a sense of possibility.

Once Mrs. Hammer had us sit on the floor with a bunch of items—glasses, hats, and some pieces of clothing—and asked us to think about how they could be woven into a story.

Another time she had us write about pictures filled to the edges with small details to hone our eyes and give us creative freedom. When I finished, I told her I would never write anything better, and she laughed, saying, "You might have peaked a little early."

One day she had the class read articles about kids like us and analyze why the authors wrote about "us" in such a way. What was their goal? How did we know?

She led us through the endless maze of Shakespeare, bringing to life difficult and massive concepts. Though I'm still a little salty about not getting the part of Romeo, as a teacher, I'm still in awe of her ability to teach something that complex so well.

Mrs. Hammer provided us with a long list of amazing activities, but the best part about being in her class was that she was 100 percent invested in all of us. She cared. She looked at us with those wide eyes of hers and took the time to see who we truly were. On the wall opposite the classroom door, the one you'd look at when you walked in, was a quote from *Hamlet* that read: "To thine own self be true." She lived that motto in her every action with us. With me.

She had skill. She had craft. She had passion. She was exactly what I needed at that time in my life, when so much was wrong and I understood so little. Her total commitment to her students is what I try to embody in my own work as a teacher. I don't think it's an overstatement to say that Hammer's class was the beginning of my future. It isn't an exaggeration to say she gave me the keys to escape my cage.

It was a sad day when I had to leave her class, but I got lucky, and she moved up to teach seniors by the time I became one (and—I'll be damned—I got the lead as Hamlet that year!).

Towards the end of senior year in Mrs. Hammer's class, we were assigned to write about our future careers. Before starting my paper, I took a career screener to see what might be a good fit. Two of those matches still stand out clearly: scientist and educator.

As I let the options percolate in my consciousness, the idea that I could become a teacher began to look more and more appealing, and more and more likely. Education had done so much for me that it was a logical focus. I chose to write my paper on becoming a professor.

Although I turned it in late, the work still holds up, in my humble opinion. At the very least, it was a wonderful snapshot of where my mind was at eighteen. There were grammar issues, some lack of control with language, and a somewhat heavy-handed approach when expressing my opinion (none of which are apparent in this book, I'm sure), but it was solid in many ways. It showed the inner workings of a kid who had been reading heavily for four years and who was starting to make sense of the chaos. It also spoke highly of Mrs. Hammer's writing instruction.

The opening paragraph of that paper reads:

> *Today, we thrive in the bliss of ignorance. We welcome with open arms the simplicity so generously offered to us by multi-billion-dollar companies. Today, we tune in to see what limelight-craving, self-distorted individual will do on a reality television show but ignore the pure and genteel author expressing the most humanistic, secular views in his writings. Today, I decide to fight, to stand against blind faith in humanity, and to jump on the frontlines to change a spiraling culture polluted by generalities. To educate and inspire awe once again in the real and most defiantly surreal world we live in.*

Other than the obvious partiality for secularism above other viewpoints, I still agree with much in this paragraph. I still believe that people are too willing to live in a state of ignorance, choosing to hide from the issues of the world behind Netflix, YouTube, Buzzfeed, and E! Online. The pursuit of knowledge has been traded for an obscene level of comfort and convenience. Too many people care about what's happening in the lives of celebrities rather than what is written in a great book or the injustices in the world, and this is a dangerous trend in a democracy.

But it's the end of the paragraph that strikes me the most. I refer to teaching as "fighting" and as "jumping on the frontlines to change a spiraling culture polluted by generalities."

An act against the problems of the world. An act against suffering.

Reading this paper today, I realize I wanted to become an educator because I wanted to "educate and inspire awe."

What?

It's amazing to me that, back in 2008-09, I was already seeing what teaching was and should be. There wasn't any mention of having the summers off, the holiday schedule, or working with kids because "I like them." I wanted to help others experience the same awe that I experienced in learning. I wanted to show learners that the world was truly amazing and that too many of us were wasting our time on earth by giving away our attention to the false idols being paraded before us like golden cattle.

In the paragraph following the introduction, I wrote:

> *I remember the first time I truly grasped how massive the universe is or how inspiring and real the words of John Adams are . . . Being thrown into a world of thought, observation, debate, writing, and hours of research would fill a desire that is as equal in size as the will to live within me.*

I'm not sure I truly grasped how large the universe is when I was eighteen (a claim that makes me laugh out loud every time I read it), but the point I was trying to make with that claim is clear: learning is just as important as the will to live. It's freedom.

Would our world be a better place if we helped young minds discover the pure joy of learning about the great facts and mysteries about our world? About our history? About music, art, science, and math? About psychology, sociology, and government? I just can't help but believe that if more young people found a joy in learning, our world's problems would feel less insurmountable.

Unfortunately, it seems our schools haven't been giving students a joy for learning. College admissions are down and have been declining for six years. Young minds are losing faith in what used to be considered the bastions of an educated society. They can't be blamed for this loss of faith, however. Public schools are so heavily focused on test prep that many teachers and administrators forget that education should be about the student, and so the student, feeling this intuitively, decides to find meaning elsewhere. Of course if they do go to college, which was once seen as the intellectual mecca for exploring minds, they find an echo chamber where ideas that disagree with the status quo are quashed by the climate of the campus. And this is all ignoring the biggest barrier and deterrent to entry: the overwhelming debt that comes along with attending these institutions.

More and more, our youngest and brightest are turning away, or are being turned away, from education in favor of another life. I believe this is directly affecting our society as a whole and allowing barriers to entry (like looming debt) and corruption of our free speech values to get worse and worse. We need more young, free, and exploring minds in schools of higher learning, not less, if we want to save our democracy and the intellect it takes for it to flourish.

I believe education is the game changer.

I'm not sure if a decade of time is considered "ages and ages hence," but I feel that when I chose the road of education, "I took the one less traveled by, and that has made all the difference." It wasn't the easiest choice, and I have faced a silencing of views and a mountain of debt afterwards, but I wouldn't change the path I took.

I was only able to do so because of the educators who guided my path.

Ten years before Hammer, there was Mrs. Hernandez, my kindergarten teacher who instilled in me a love for school, encouraged my creativity, and showed us that all cultures have something valuable to offer by teaching us both English and Spanish. There was Mrs. Coffee, one of the sweetest teachers I've ever known. She sang with us, engaged us, and cared about our stories and lives. She read to us from *Where the Red Fern Grows* as we sat on the carpet around her and cried at the end of the year as she finished the story and closed the book. Mrs. Urban, the toughest elementary teacher I had, taught me discipline, pushed me to write neatly, and taught me how to separate myself from the problems in my life. She taught me about the "cloud" that protected me for so many years.

In the fourth and fifth grades, there was Mr. Hansen, who taught me the power of history and seeing the importance of respecting those who've come before us. He taught me that science is worth knowing and that it exposes us to the mysteries of our vast universe. He taught me to revisit my fiction and add the details that would help the reader visualize what I was writing. He taught me that it's cool to like weird music, fantasy books, and science fiction. Reading to us from *The Hobbit*, doing Gollum's voice long before it was a thing, he would command all of my attention, and my eyes would never leave him or the illustrated version of the book he was holding.

Along with Mrs. Hammer in high school, I had Mr. McNulty and Mr. Blackard, my drum directors. They were father figures to me when my own father was busy living in motels, getting fired from jobs, and slowly falling into a cycle of homelessness and jail. My band director, Mr. Watson, always pushed us to be the best musicians we could be. When we fell short of his expectations— and our abilities—we ran a lap around the school. He cared for us more than I knew at the time.

I could continue to list teachers. I could tell you about Mrs. Morgan, who exposed me to classic literature and saw that my willingness to debate was a skill, not a class distraction. I could share about the many math teachers who spent time with me when I had no idea what was going on.

So many of these educators gave me their time and attention and truly made a difference in the trajectory of my life.

All of them, every name I've mentioned along with those I haven't, served as the human building blocks of my love of learning. They fed my desire to work tirelessly to help young minds realize that their world is beautiful, learning is fulfilling, and taking the road less traveled, the road paved with a passion for education and learning, is always a better choice.

Teach Students for Who They Can Be

I was a drummer in the marching band in high school, and I was solid. In the words of my drum director, Mr. McNulty, I was "hella talented."

He would always say that after getting frustrated with me for not doing what I was supposed to. The follow-up was usually something like, ". . . but I need you to learn your part," or, ". . . but you need to be able to read music better."

I had played music my whole life and had grown up watching my dad play a massive red Ludwig drum set with eight toms, auxiliary percussion instruments, and more cymbals than I could realistically spend money on now. It was heaven for a kid learning, and I learned all I could.

What I developed was an ear for music and rhythm. I couldn't tell you I was playing in 5/4, but I could do it. I couldn't tell you I was using sixteenth notes and triplets, but I was able to. I learned to turn on the radio and absorb the music, seeing the beats in my head, and then I would go out to the garage, turn up our old PA system, and jam out for all the neighbors to hear.

I played religiously. By the time books took over my life, music was already an old friend. When my parents fought, I went to the garage and drowned them out with Metallica. When my mom was too messed up to talk, I took my anger out to the garage and played until it was too late or until I couldn't play anymore. And when I just felt like being with music—all those bands and songs and burned CDs that spoke to me and healed me—I would go sit at that drum set and just be.

That drum set taught me a lot about life. I learned that dedication, practice, work, and sweat could lead to results. I learned that music could save me from whatever issue I was having. Playing in the garage, I was rarely bothered, and it became my sanctuary, my chapel.

It's not hard to see why my drum director had to have "the talk" with me several times a month. Either he didn't understand why I chose not to learn certain pieces of music, or he did and thought he could steer me in the right direction. Perhaps he just didn't have time to give me what I needed. I resisted learning to read music because I didn't want it to steal the magic of what was happening in my head. I didn't want to be told what to play; I just wanted to play what I felt, what I loved, and I didn't waiver.

At the time I thought these were excellent reasons.

Have you ever had a student like me, a kid you knew was "hella talented"? A kid who was ridiculously smart, clever, funny, athletic, or gifted in a particular subject, but also kind of a pain in the neck?

All we want to do for these students is show them how great they are. We want to help them see that if they could just focus, if they could just do the assignment, if they could just learn that lame (sorry, McNulty) piece of music, they could do some great things.

My drum directors and my band director knew more about my home life than my other teachers in high school. They counseled me when I needed it, picked me up and drove me to practice, and threw me more bones than I could count. When I needed encouragement, they pulled me aside and offered it. When I was being an idiot, they told me. When my mom was in jail and I was driving to school on Mother's Day morning and totaled my mom's car, they were the ones who picked me up afterwards and made sure I still got to school that day. I'm sure they saw a kid that had a lot of talent. They thought if I could only, you know, do what was asked of me, then I would be great and have a better life. They tried their hardest to get me there.

As a teacher now, I know they were doing the one thing they could do to help a kid who was, honestly, making stupid decisions—they were choosing to push me in the right direction.

When I see students in situations similar to mine or worse, I can't help but wonder if this is how we should be reaching out to them.

Mr. McNulty eventually ran out of patience and demoted me to help me "learn a lesson," but kicking me off of the drumline my senior year didn't make me realize my mistakes. It took me out of one of the safest places I had as a teenager. Putting me in a lower band ranking because I wouldn't learn songs on marimba and because I struggled with passing classes didn't make me learn marimba or pass those classes. It turned one of my favorite activities into a dull and boring chore.

I don't blame him in the slightest for his decisions. I understand them, especially as a teacher today, but I've spent time reflecting on them, and I wonder if they were the most effective way to help me.

I've reacted the same way in my classroom. I've had kids who are great thinkers and have punished them when they don't do the work, which inspires anything but a desire to do the work. In my early days of teaching English, I punished kids for not wanting to read by forcing them to read more of what they didn't want to read.

And what did I solve? Did I capture the thinker? Did I inspire the reader who was bored with what I'd chosen? No. I didn't change them. I satisfied a misguided desire to "fix" these students. I was so focused on getting results that I forgot to look at what those results would cost.

We have all done this at some point, and some of us are still doing it.

We stick to the ritual of work: "I assigned it; therefore, you must do it. That's how this relationship runs. If you dare color outside of the lines I've provided, there will be consequences. If you dare get distracted and think about something that's more interesting than a vocabulary assignment, you're in the wrong and will be punished accordingly!"

What a dull way to teach.

These kids who sit in our classes have a variety of needs, many of which a teacher cannot meet. We can't give them a loving home or a childhood free of violence or drug abuse.

What we can do is be better at our jobs for their sakes.

How amazing would it be for those students—those like me, who show so much promise but lack focus—if we were smarter than the problem? Rather than punishing the talented musician for not learning a piece of music, why not ask her what she would like to learn and challenge her to push her skill to the next level? Rather than punishing students for being bored with the book you selected, give them a few choices and see what they choose to read. If we are truly skilled in our craft and practices, then we can teach them using whatever text resonates with them.

Today they might resist the assignment, lesson, or task, but if we meet them where they are and if we remember they are a work in progress, we can help them reach a future they see as worth having. In some ways it requires teaching the students for who they can be, not who they are today.

I didn't refuse to learn pieces of music because I hated band; I refused because I had a passion in me that was wild and untamed. I didn't see how those pieces would benefit me, but I didn't have a lack of desire. The desire was just pointed elsewhere.

That's what many of our frustrating students are like. They don't want to be difficult; they just don't understand how to channel all of their greatness. On the flip side, many teachers don't want to hurt a child's passion, but they aren't comfortable deviating from their lesson plans and state standards. In this situation the responsibility falls to teachers to be adaptive, creative, and sensitive to these students' particular needs and interests.

Teaching is powerful. Teaching is difficult. It's as fun as it is frustrating and as cyclical as it is fluid. Most of all, teaching is needed.

We must teach students for who they can be, not who they are today.

The unexpected Happens

At the end of my first year of teaching, I was finally getting into a groove. Although I was fighting a lot of the bad habits I had instilled in my students, we were making progress. Lessons were going well, and I was starting to design them with engagement—and not my own ego—in mind. Using fewer of my partner's lesson plans, I began to spread my wings and develop my educator's voice. Life was good.

My teaching partner and I were looking forward to doing great things with year two. She was excited about the idea of keeping the same partner for more than a year, which hadn't happened in the last six, and I was excited to start a new year with my newfound skills. It was going to be great knowing the curriculum moving into my second year. Having content knowledge is far different from knowing the scope and sequence of a school, not to mention all of the different skills we are required to teach within each standard.

A couple weeks before the school year started, I was invited to meet with our new principal.

Well, shit.

I quickly texted my partner, and she pretty much echoed those thoughts.

We knew what was coming—change, alternative plans, total derailment!

The meeting was less awkward than we thought it would be. Our new principal happened to be one of my high school teachers, Mr. Whitfield, so we already had a relationship to some degree and chatted a bit before getting down to business.

"Now, if I've been told correctly, you would be interested in teaching ELA," he said.

Small heart sink. "I would," I conceded. "Who told you that?"

Mrs. Hammer, the same Mrs. Hammer who taught me in high school and who was also the assistant principal at my school at the time, had mentioned it to him before moving on to her new campus.

"Ah," I said. "Well, yes. I would like to teach ELA."

"Well, I have a position open in sixth-grade ELA for you. I'd like to have someone with experience in the position, and I think you're a good fit for the job."

This could have been an issue, but it really wasn't. I didn't want to leave my partner or social studies, but my love for literature was far greater than my love for history. History is important, but ELA is timeless. Reading literature, studying poetry, learning how to read and critique expository texts, and just digging into the power of language—for me, that's where the magic is. I had a choice, but it wasn't really a choice. The universe seemed to be doing its thing in my life again.

To be honest, I had more reservations about moving to sixth grade than to ELA. ELA was an easy choice, but I wasn't sure how I would feel about teaching younger kids. In my visions of teaching, I had always imagined myself in high school. When I got my middle school position, it was because of circumstance, not necessarily by choice. I quickly grew to love eighth-graders, but I wasn't sure it would happen with my sixth-graders too.

Shifting to sixth grade was a big change, and it was awfully close to the start of the new school year, but I embraced my new path, both nervous and excited about the possibilities. All of my favorite teachers had been ELA teachers. It was time to see behind the curtain.

I came home from the meeting and told my wife I was going to teach ELA that year. She was shocked and excited for me. As usual, we both sat down and examined everything we could about the position. Our voices became increasingly excited as we looked over the standards for sixth-grade ELA and realized this was the best possible position I could be in. It was perfect.

At that time, my school split ELA into separate writing and reading classes. I was on the reading side. This meant all of my standards were about reading skills, inferencing, and the like. Compared to the massive number of standards in eighth-grade social studies, the reading standards seemed too few. It was a bit disorienting.

Sitting in my department chair's class a few weeks later, staring at the standards and supporting documents provided by the district, I wondered aloud where all of the "stuff" was.

"Where is the stuff we teach?" I asked.

"What do you mean? It's right there," she answered, giving me a not-so-subtle side-eye.

"Yeah, but what do we teach? What do we read?"

"You have to find it."

Cue dramatic theme music!

Social studies, you must understand, was a relatively clear path. When it says to teach your kids about Jamestown, you do just that. (This is clearly a gross oversimplification for the sake of my upcoming point. I just want to convey that social studies standards in Texas are clearer and more defined than many of the standards in the ELA curriculum.) When the ELA standards say to teach students to infer and support their conclusions from a variety of texts, you must do the research to select texts that will work for your classes. In my district we have a few common texts and novels built into the curriculum we must teach, but not many.

Although it was initially a shock, I ultimately loved the freedom. English and literature were greater passions of mine than history, but all I had in my toolbox was a natural sense of how to teach them. I had a whole lot of instinct because I was a voracious reader, and I had some really great English teachers to emulate, but I didn't have many solid, proven practices to hold on to. I didn't go to school to teach. My first degree was in communications. Everything I had learned in my first year was all I knew about teaching, but not everything learned in one subject is easily transferred to another, especially when teaching students how to read, write, and think.

I had a feeling we should be reading engaging texts of all kinds, but I didn't know how to select and teach those texts in a pedagogically sophisticated way. I didn't know what a reader's workshop was or how to use independent reading to engage reluctant readers. Hell, I didn't even know how to teach students to read more carefully.

I was essentially a new teacher again. With a few ideas about how to teach the standards—albeit with massive gaps in my knowledge—I was firmly back in my ideals and outside of reality. I also didn't have a partner to lean on. My grade-level partner was a first-year teacher (who was far more amazing than I was during my first year, by the way), and my department head, though a close friend, didn't see eye to eye with me on many things. That meant I spent a lot of time figuring things out on my own, exploring, having fun, and failing—a lot.

It wasn't a total reset, however. I had some classroom management skills, knew what a quiet signal was and how to teach it, and knew that kids needed structure and procedure. I counted on those pieces while I scrambled to learn how to further the massive cause we call *literacy*.

If my first year of teaching was a whirlwind of a hurricane with spots of bright sunshine, my second year was a thunderstorm with long periods of spring.

And did I have some fun along the way!

I think teachers are too willing to beat themselves up for not being perfect in their classrooms. If they go a day or more not truly knowing how they will get their students from point A to point B, they allow self-loathing and doubt to creep into their mindsets. We know teaching is an important job, and many of us start to believe the myth that it's entirely on us to raise our students to new heights, that it's our responsibility alone to bring our students out of the darkness of their own youth.

That's just not the case!

We often forget that learning isn't exact, and teachers and their lesson plans don't need to be perfect for learning to occur. I would argue that it's probably better if our classrooms aren't perfect all of the time (though let's not confuse imperfection with ineptitude).

In many circles of thought, the teacher remains the arbiter of knowledge, yet study after study has revealed that children— when given the right space to explore and experiment and work with each other—develop in beautiful ways on their own. This is especially true for younger and struggling students. Teachers are facilitators of learning. We don't show up to give learning; we show up to allow learning to occur.

Our classrooms don't need to be these neat and tidy environments for learning to happen. If we have put in the work to make our classrooms places that inspire learning, then we can have off days when we aren't exact in our teaching and be okay with it. It's going to happen. You can either stress about it and beat yourself up or accept it as part of the process. If our classrooms give kids choices and spaces to explore and we have set up norms and procedures and a culture that leads to mutual respect, the learning will happen. To make up for those off days you're all sure to have, create a classroom in which your students can experience authentic, self-directed learning instead of simply absorbing your personal genius as a teacher.

This was incredibly hard for me to do my second year. Truthfully, it was my biggest weakness. I was still very much a direct teacher, meaning I stood up, talked about language and character and plot and persuasion, and then sent my students off to work on some passage with questions attached. I tried finding interesting passages, but the teaching moves, lesson, and task left a lot to be desired.

It wasn't until after Christmas break that I started providing more choices in the work my students did. I began experimenting with new structures, such as allowing my students to read for fifteen minutes at the beginning of class and then reflect on their personal reading and the reading we were doing as a class. I dabbled in conferring. I started to let go of total control of the learning and listened to what they wanted to do, explore, and read about.

I thought about my best teachers, the Mr. Hansens and Mrs. Hammers. I knew I needed more choice, more discovery, and more authentic tasks for my students. I saw what I was doing and realized I needed to grow. I began examining my practices deeply as the year went on, watching my moves and thinking about what didn't work. I stood in my room and looked at my students working and asked myself over and over again, "Would I want to be a student in my class right now?" If the answer was no, then I changed what I was doing.

As time went on, my students began to enjoy my class more. Their learning was deeper and they progressed faster. I began to feel a deep fulfillment in my day-to-day work in the classroom. There is a satisfaction that comes with reading workshop and inquiry-based learning. I wasn't fully there, but the feeling was beginning to swell around me. I was starting to get on the right track.

As I moved to this style of teaching, I began realizing that the classroom was much more about my students than myself. If I set it up just right and directed my students in the right ways to pursue their interests, I didn't need to be perfect all the time. The stress of feeling the weight of my job and its importance began to wane as I realized learning happens where learning is fostered. A teacher still needs to be present to encourage, direct, and guide, but the learning can occur even if the teacher is having an off day.

This became the vision and the drive of my professional development. More and more I would hone these ideas as best I could and see where the path took my classes.

Teachers can't always be "on." We can't always be the best teacher with the best lessons. Life happens—a death in the family, shaky finances, a fight with a spouse, a check-engine light. But if we have put in the early work of creating classrooms that foster learning, even when we are struggling, we will see the success we all wish for our students.

The unexpected happens. That's when the fun begins.

— Lesson 13 —

Passion Is a Form of Pain

The Latin root of passion is *pati*, which means to suffer or to endure. Passion, in its simplest form, refers to a type of pain that needs to be healed, fixed, or resolved.

As someone who lived in pain for many years, I find this fascinating. Passion drives me to be a great father, a great husband, and a great educator. Passion drives me to keep pushing and evolving. It drives me to get better.

I'm struck that as we feel passion for something, true passion, we are literally living with a form of pain that craves to be remedied or healed, and that craving propels us forward.

Everyone has heard the saying that love hurts, but the truth is that love heals, while passion hurts. The passion we feel for our spouses can cause us to hurt, to desire so much that we literally keep pushing—burning—until the pain has been consumed and released in its entirety. Perhaps this is why some people are obsessed with someone for a period of time before suddenly breaking it off. They burned up their passion. They stopped hurting so they could heal.

Passion cannot last by itself. It will crumble under the pressure because passion is selfish. All it wants is to be healed. If passion is the foundation of the work you do, then your dedication and intention, your hard work, must be the rebar that holds it all together. Passion and hard work must work in tandem and balance each other, because an imbalance creates a loss of opportunity for the magic that school and learning can be.

I've seen teachers do their work to the best of their ability with great intention and dedication to their craft. No one could or would say that they're bad or ineffective teachers, but many of these hard-working teachers fail at creating the magic students need to be driven to do great things. Their students might understand math, but do they *care* about it? They might be able to infer specific meanings from any text, but do they *love* reading? They might be able to answer a multiple-choice question about American Reconstruction, but do they truly *feel the weight* of that era, what it meant for the people of the time and what it means now? Hard work can get our content into students' heads, but it doesn't create a love for and deep understanding of all our fantastic subjects of study. I believe the world is too beautiful to treat learning about it as just a means to pass a test or make a 100 on an assignment. To get our students to that next level of care, we have to bring our passion to the class.

However, many people argue that it's a teacher's job to teach content, not teach a love for the content. They say it doesn't matter if the students find a love for the content of the class. At the end of the day, in public education, our job is to get kids to a certain level for them to pass a test and move on to the next grade.

The thing is, those teachers are right. In most public schools, we simply don't have time to teach a love for books or a love for the scientific method. We must teach standards. There is a very real job we have to do, and it isn't all sunshine and rainbows.

This isn't about teaching, though. Passionate teachers don't teach a love for science; they reveal its power. They show students their own fire and curiosity and interest in science. Passionate teachers don't teach a love for math; they inspire kids to discover how math can unlock the secrets of the world. Passionate teachers don't teach a love for reading and writing; they empower students to become independent readers and writers. They model. Combine this with hard work and dedication to the craft and art of teaching, and you have a special educator. It's what we should all strive to be.

Passion is infectious. As human beings, we're wired to feel each other's pain. When we're around people who are passionate, we can feel the warmth emanating from their very souls. It's why we can find ourselves attracted to people or videos discussing topics that we aren't typically interested in. We're attracted to their passion, and if we're around it long enough, we just might develop a new interest.

As mentioned earlier, passion is pain, and that cannot be ignored. Passion is a state of desire. If you're passionate about teaching, then, in a way, you're in pain unless you're teaching. You have to do it, or you're simply unhappy.

I experience this in my own life. I have a passion for teaching, a desire to teach young people the wonders of reading and writing. I feel like less of a person when I'm not in the classroom, even when we're on break for a holiday. My desire to teach, to be amid the day-in and day-out grind of it all, is so great that it's literally like being away from a loved one when I'm not in the classroom.

As I work through my master's program, a dual degree in curriculum and instruction and educational leadership, I find myself paying closer attention to how my school operates. I watch how teachers react to campus or school district news being delivered in certain ways. I try to sense the pulse of the school. *What makes it beat faster? What slows it down?* I watch the teachers. They are the lifeblood of a school, after all. Without teachers the building is nothing more than a jail for students. Teachers make or break a school. They can be empowered to do their best work or stifled until they're broken.

I love watching all sorts of teachers. Some have been in the profession so long that they have forgotten more than I've learned. Others are beaten down. Many are still pushing themselves to try new things. Some go with the flow, and a few buck the system. Some follow, some lead. And some, the passionate and hard-working ones, change the lives of their students for the better. Walking into their classrooms is like a revelation.

As a leader, if I had to choose between the two, I would take a passionate teacher over a teacher with the best scores any day. Scores do a lot. They reflect accountability, they keep schools funded, and they get district officials out of your hair. What they don't do is inspire students to achieve greater things, the stuff that breathes life back into the world.

Quality teachers with high scores can help make a school good, but passionate teachers make a school great. A school filled with teachers who achieve high scores will look good on paper and appease some of the powers that control our schools, but what are they really doing? Are they inspiring our next leaders, or are they teaching kids to study for a test? Do the kids acing the ELA exams have a passion to keep reading when they're adults, or will they drop the habit as soon as there is no score attached to the task?

Of course, good scores and a deep passion for teaching are not mutually exclusive; it's just something we have to consider, regardless of whether we are looking at a campus as a leader or if we are reflecting on our own classroom. Our kids may be performing well on assessments, but are they also continuing their search into the content areas on their own? Are we making good test-takers, or are we helping them find deep meaning in the subjects that bond humanity together?

Many students have great scores in school. So what? What are they doing now, as an adult, in their twenties? Thirties? Forties?

I know a lot of people who earned excellent scores in school. They were at the top of their classes. Now they do nothing of significance. They flounder in real life because they learned the game of education rather than the passion of education. They did what they had to do in order to "win" at school, but the problem is that the skills necessary for that don't always translate to real life.

I fundamentally believe a passion for education and teaching is one of the most vital skills a teacher can have because it will bind them to their students and inspire those students to learn beyond the grades and the assignments. If we are talking about setting up our students for an amazing life outside of the walls of our campuses, and I hope we are, then this should be our primary goal.

Was I a great student? Not at all, but I had passionate teachers who taught me how and why to love education. Almost every year I was in school, I had at least one teacher who was driven with passion, and it fed into me.

I didn't do that well on my state tests, but I'm an avid adult reader.

I didn't do well in math, but I value the world math has given us and the thinking it inspires.

I didn't know every person in history and their significance, yet I absorbed why it's important to not only know history but also apply its lessons in my daily life.

Because of my teachers, I am successful in spite of all of the abuse, fear, and rage I experienced growing up. They were passionate and hard-working, and their passion fueled my own. They showed me there are greater things to desire than drugs, suffering, and drama. They showed me that education is an endless well of possibilities. I latched on to that, and my adult life was literally transformed by it.

I see people my age, many of them my friends, and they're just drifting through life doing a whole lot of nothing. They weren't inspired to go to college. Many of them haven't read a book since high school or before. They change jobs every few months or years, and I just can't help but wonder how their lives might be different if they had been taught by some of my teachers. Would they be doing more? Would they be achieving their dreams instead of just talking about them over beers? I hate to see people struggling to find focus and meaning. Life is too important to waste like this. It's one of my greatest fears as a teacher that my students will grow up directionless. I'm not saying you always have to know where you are going in life. Not all who wander are lost, after all, but a wanderer can still walk with a purpose.

What about the few friends who had the same teachers I had? We were in the same classes. Why didn't they absorb the passion I did? How can some of our students become passionate about learning while others just slip right on through, never latching on to it, no matter how passionate we are about our content and craft?

I think the answer isn't that a student should have one great passionate teacher; they should have many, over and over and over again. It isn't enough for a student to have one great teacher; they need to be surrounded by them. It isn't enough for a campus to have one all-star; it needs to be an entire campus of all-stars.

Passionate teachers can change the lives of their students, and they can help mold a school into a place of authentic and deep work, into a place of unending passionate joy.

Passion is a form of pain, but pain can be a good thing. Pain can drive us, change us, and push us to be better.

As I moved through my second year of teaching and navigated the new world of ELA, I had a lot of passion. Because of that, I had a lot of great people offer assistance. They saw that I wasn't having the most success, but I had passion and a willingness to learn and grow.

And then one day, my friend, a literacy specialist at my school, sat me down to discuss what would later become the foundation for my classroom for years to come. She saw my focus and desire to better my teaching and showed me a door I didn't know existed. Through the door was the work of Donalyn Miller and Kelly Gallagher, which would expose me to many other great thinkers and thought leaders in literacy education, all of which would help me bring my practices to the next level.

— Lesson 14 —

Books Are Powerful

My mom was reading on our large, gray, sectional couch. The sun had set, and the warm air was cooling around the pecan trees outside. Dinner had been served and eaten, yet the smell of Hamburger Helper and mashed potatoes still lingered in the air. She was reading *A Child Called "It": One Child's Courage to Survive* and playfully said that the mother in the book had some "good ideas." (If you don't know what this book is about, do a quick Amazon search for it.)

I was on the couch nearby, cozy under a blanket, watching her read.

After a time, I got up, went to my room, found my novelization of the *Rugrats* movie, and came back to sit on the couch where I had been. I wasn't the strongest reader at the time, which, based on the publishing date of the *Rugrats* book, was when I was around the age of eight. I remember not being able to read the book until a while after we bought it. My eyes would instead drift to the pictures that were at the center of the novel.

Because my reading skill wasn't up to par for that book, what I spent a lot of time doing that night was pretending to read. Even if I couldn't read the book, I wanted to *look* like a reader. I remember asking my mom before I was even in kindergarten, "When will I learn to read?"

Just seeing an adult in my life read a book, even sparsely, made me want to do it. Before I ever discovered the power of narrative, I wanted to be involved in the world of books. Long before I fell in love with story and characters, I loved sitting with a book. It was as if I knew the doors to my home life's escape hatch were near, but I didn't yet know how to open them. This fact is amazing to me, and it's a fact that has driven me to model being a reader to my students. We can never be sure what kids are getting from us, but we can be sure they are getting *something* from us. Always.

My mom eventually stopped reading books and stopped modeling behaviors that would benefit me as a growing child, but it was because of her I had my first bookshelf to explore.

Our living room was a dark thing with only one large window to illuminate the long, wood-paneled walls. Off in the corner, just to the right of the entertainment center, was a shelving area built into the wall. This is where my mom stashed her modest selection of books. Most of them were older novels. I remember grabbing Dean Koontz and Stephen King. There were several Oprah-style religious books, as well as several books whose covers I can still see in my mind but whose titles and authors I can't recall. There was a thick Dr. Seuss collection too, a rainbow among the dirty and faded covers.

I didn't read many of these old books, but I explored them. I picked them up when I was bored, curious as to what they might be able to do for me. I read parts of them and took some to my room and examined them (a habit I still have).

My wife makes fun of me for how often I'll sit on our bed and just stare at our floor-to-ceiling bookshelf. She groans when she sees a stack of books I've taken down in the middle of the night after she's gone to sleep, knowing I'm not actually re-reading any of them, just exploring and remembering them like old friends, just being comfortable in their presence.

Not enough can be said about the nature of being around books and how that proximity can change the life of a child. We easily accept this when we talk about drugs and violence. Most people nod in approval when we talk about the cyclical nature of those social ills, but few ever stop to think about books in the same way.

Proximity to books also played a role in my life while I was at school.

I have vivid memories of sitting in my fifth-grade class during Drop Everything and Read time, watching kids read these massive books I couldn't yet read myself. They were reading the fourth *Harry Potter* book, *The Lord of the Rings* series, novelizations of *Star Wars: The Clone Wars*, and *Redwall*. All kinds of great books. Books I couldn't power through yet. Books I wanted more than anything to read because they were big and powerful and offered something I just knew I needed.

I wasn't a bad reader; I just hadn't matured to the point of being able to tackle a tome. This is where I get to thank the writers of books like *Hank the Cowdog*, *Captain Underpants*, and *Goosebumps*. Without these books, I might never have had the success I needed to become an independent reader just a few years later. I remind myself of this every time I see a child pick up *Dork Diaries*, *Diary of a Wimpy Kid*, or the *Amulet* series for the hundredth time. Without these great gateways to literature, how many students would we never reach with the power of reading? It breaks me a little when I see teachers scoff at these book selections. Every book has the power to change us. Every book has the power to give a child a love for reading.

But even as I tackled these smaller (but great) children's books, I was still sitting with big books. I loved to hold them. They were, and still are, like massive worlds that promised a different reality. At home I would be scared another fight would break out, but in a book, I was tasked with taking down the evil sorcerer, killing the monster, or simply having a great adventure. The bigger the book, the longer I could stay away from the world I had to live in every day. The bigger the book, the bigger the promise.

Years later, after my family fell apart and my dad left my mom for another woman to try to escape the debt that was chasing him, I was alone a lot. My mom would be at a bar, and I'd be in an apartment with little to do but read. Long novels, many of them the same novels I couldn't read but wanted to as a child, let me travel into fantastical lands and walk among heroes who lived for something greater than themselves. I was alone in a rocking chair as the sun set, but I was fighting off the evil forces of the world with Eragon, Frodo, and Harry Potter.

As a teacher, I get kids who come to my classroom who love to read, kids who read when they are asked and like it, kids who read when they are asked and hate it, and kids who resist it entirely. Each kid is at a different reading level. Just because they find reading boring doesn't mean they read at a low level, and just because they love it doesn't mean they are particularly great readers.

It is my job to work with my readers where they are. My end goal is to have them become strong, independent readers. I want them to love reading and see value in it.

A love for reading will increase the likelihood that they will become independent readers, and it will also continue to serve them in life as they read works of greater complexity, explore new avenues of literature, and learn about themselves as human beings. They will be able to work their way through the complicated world of human interaction and emotions, the world of contracts, and the democratic process.

By meeting them where they are, supporting their choices in book selection, and supporting their interests, I stand to make a greater impact on their reading lives than the teacher pushing students to be a certain kind of reader. I'm not pushing them to be readers who only read high-level material or readers who see books only as doorways to more worksheets.

I'll be honest here. I started in ELA with the goal of exposing my students to the books I valued and the books I figured a literary society would value. With that mindset, however, I lost far more ground than I gained. By pushing certain works on my young readers—many of whom came with limited reading lives—I was running the risk of destroying their love for reading. I wasn't pushing great and challenging pieces of literature based on student interest and desire, which would have been ideal; I was pushing books I valued simply because I valued them and not because they were the most appropriate books for my students to be reading.

I would love to have every student read *Of Mice and Men*, *The Great Gatsby*, *Moby Dick*, or *Great Expectations*, but many aren't ready for these books or even interested in them at all, just like we weren't in school. We were forced to read these books, and many of us came out with a strong hatred for them, despite their timeless beauty and endless applicability to our lives.

What a terrible cost to pay to have any of these books be hated just because a teacher showed them off too early out of some overzealous ambition to expose his students to the literary canon.

In my own reading life, I didn't care about any of these classics until I rediscovered them on my own as an adult. *Great Expectations* has become a book that I consider life-changing (though the original ending is better, I have to say). I thought it was incredibly boring as a teenager. I wasn't forced to read *Moby Dick*, but I had a teacher in high school talk at length about how much she loved the book. When I came across it and tried it organically, I had a natural interest in it and found that I loved it as well.

Choice is powerful. Being ready is powerful. Many schools and classrooms have continued to treat school with a factory mindset, repeating the same basic and sterile processes, thinking it will churn out quality academics. Many like to pretend like we're free and open to new ideas, but many of us feel physical fear when we throw out old ideas for the new. This fear characterizes many well-meaning ELA teachers.

I can lovingly criticize educators that try to push certain types of literature or beliefs about how students can show mastery of "knowledge" because I was one of them. When I started teaching ELA, I had no true concept of what independent reading looked like or how to get students to be independent readers. I didn't know how to get kids to write authentic pieces in writer's workshop or teach with the stories they wanted to read and explore. I knew great classic books, and I tried to show them to my students. It worked for some but not most. I got a lot of students into books I consider to be the best of their genre, but I left a lot of other students floundering with books they didn't enjoy or, worse, couldn't see themselves in because of a lack of diversity. I gave multiple-choice tests based on those books that didn't accurately tell me what students knew, just who could take that particular test well or who sort of paid attention to whole-class novel studies.

All of this was true until my friend and co-worker, a reading specialist in every sense of the word, sat me down and gave me two books—*The Book Whisperer* by Donalyn Miller and *Readicide* by Kelly Gallagher—that would change my life forever.

Both of these books suggest approaching reading instruction with the student in mind, not the teacher. They tell us that if we want readers in our classrooms, then we can't take the essential pieces of being a reader out of the equation. We can't take away choice, because readers thrive when they are given a choice of what to read. Readers thrive when they have the freedom to abandon books if they choose one they don't enjoy. Readers thrive when they get to take part in authentic conversations about books or respond to a piece of text out of their own desire to do so and not because it's a graded assignment.

We can't force students into a certain academic box with reading; we must meet them where they are. A non-reader isn't going to respond to being forced to read a dense classic they can't relate to or access. They will play the game of school (if they care about grades) and then move on, often hating some of those books in the process.

If we can't find time to teach books and give our students the freedom to choose the books they want to explore—and fill our libraries with books that connect to every kind of kid, whether that's rich, poor, straight, gay, trans, black, white, Muslim, or Christian—then we don't have time to do our jobs. We can't teach worksheets and passages for the sake of test prep. The students in our classrooms deserve better.

If ELA teachers aren't using their class time to allow children to read, explore, and interact with books in an authentic manner, then they are wasting those precious minutes. It isn't enough to give your students one day a week to read; we must give them time to read every single day.

After I read *The Book Whisperer* over a weekend, I showed up Monday morning with a new class schedule. I had looked at everything I was doing, identified all the times when students weren't reading in my space, and I changed things up! Not because the book told me to, but because it made sense.

The work Donalyn and Kelly put together in *The Book Whisperer*, *Readicide*, and their later works centers on the latest research regarding what helps improve our students as readers and puts into words how readers think and act. When I read those books, I reflected on myself as a reader, and I realized my teaching practices weren't in line with what readers need. My "bell ringer," a daily quote we discuss, was less effective than fifteen minutes of independent reading. Worksheets weren't as engaging as looking at books and model texts they cared about.

Because I was still learning in my second year, I was teaching my reading class as if they weren't readers. I was using outdated practices because those practices were what I had at the time.

Halfway into the year, I completely reformed my class structure to incorporate independent reading for fifteen minutes at the beginning of every class and based more tasks on authentic texts chosen by students. I wasn't the best at this, but I knew it was the way I needed to go, and I leaned on the research conducted by a host of experts, including Donalyn Miller, Kelly Gallagher, Penny Kittle, Terry Lesene, Mary Howard, Laura Robb, Regie Routman, Donald Graves, Donald Murray, and Nancy Atwell.

My beliefs and practices changed from a school-work mentality to a student mentality.

These educators taught me that if you let students read authentically, their skills as readers will increase, and they will slowly get receptive to what we have to offer them through the powerful lessons we design. If we meet them where they are and attend to what they need now, we will slowly build them up to have the skills to dissect more complicated texts. But if we push certain books too early, which many middle and high schools do, we hurt our readers. It doesn't matter if a high school student should be able to read

1984 and understand all of the information and story in the book; it matters if they can. As English teachers, it's our job to know our students and teach for what they need. The students come first, not the content.

Giving students autonomy over their reading doesn't mean the teacher isn't there to make executive decisions. While I find it immensely beneficial to let my sixth-graders choose what they want to read, give them that wonderful reading time, and conference with them weekly, I also find it helpful to use model texts with them. Reading one book as a touchstone, one book of their choice, and a shorter work all in the same week is one of the best ways to teach content and meet our students where they are.

As a teacher at a Title 1 school, I get kids from all kinds of backgrounds. Many come from families who read and encourage learning, but many don't. My classes start off with roughly 70 percent of students having a less-than-substantial reading life. They have reading moments, but almost all of those occur at school. The only books they've ever known are the books that line the shelves in their teachers' classrooms and in the school library. The only books they've ever gotten to the end of are the books the teachers finished or audiobooks they heard played for the whole class.

And when they step into my classroom and see my library with its chairs, bean bags, rug, and shelves and shelves of books, they flock to them. How couldn't they? The books are calling to them, screaming to be held. The books are color coded (to show genre, not levels), which strikes an interest in the minds of young people. What do the colors mean? Many are facing out, and they get explored first. Many students locate the genre chart to orient themselves to the colors, while others just wander and look at each one. Feeling them. Many students find something they like and hold it. When I ask them if they'd like to take it home to read, their eyes light up, unsure if I'm joking or not.

I reassure them that I'm serious. I let my students read and take books at will. I tell them that if they find something they like, by all means, they should go read it! If they hate the book they've been reading for fifteen minutes, they should change it! No one has time for bad books.

Throughout the year, I'll say over and over again, "If you're bored with your book, you're reading a book that is bad for you, and no one has time for that. Get another."

And they do.

As I watch my students get books, try them, and put them back, I start to notice the ones who never stick with anything, who look lost in the library, or who clearly select a book at random. I spend a lot of time with these students. We talk about what they like and what they don't like. I repeatedly reassure them that it's okay if they don't like anything yet. Many of these reluctant readers are so used to being punished for not reading that they just try to fake-read the best they know how. Books are a vast land undiscovered by many, and I assure them we will keep exploring together. We will keep learning this new world. I pair them with students who've already drawn personal maps of the landscape, which helps. I sit with them. Making stacks of possible options, I assign what I call "book tutorials." We explore the school library together, always on the lookout for a book that piques their interest. I allow my knowledge and passion for literature to flow out as we explore, making sure I'm as well read in books for my students as possible so that when I'm walking the land with them, I know where to guide them.

Imagine if I just forced this kind of student into a box by handing them a book and saying, "We are all reading this, so you have to as well." Would I have made gains with that student? Possibly. There is a time and a place for whole-class novels, but we must weigh the cost. Not every student will love or care about the whole-class book. Reading a text as a class can be a calculated move, but it must not be the only calculated move we make.

If I want my students to read the greatest works of fiction, I need them to be confident in their reading and trust that I respect their autonomy as individuals. If we can get there, then we can show them the depths of literature. If we push too soon, they'll get lost, and they'll find themselves wandering alone forever, eventually hating the land that offers so much possibility.

A lot of my time these days is spent putting books in kids' hands. I want students who have a shallow reading life to touch as many books as possible. I want them to smell them. To explore. To feel. To open and close. To flip through the pages. To see the different fonts and paper types. I want them to realize that the backs of books aren't always where you find descriptions—and that some don't have descriptions at all! I want them to be absorbed in books so that they gain confidence. I want them to learn about the possibilities that books offer. I want them to experience loving a character, becoming friends with a character, unknowingly developing personality traits from the characters, feeling heartbreak over the death of a loved character, wanting to reread books again so they can hang out with their old friends one more time, and finding Easter eggs in different books by the same author. I want them to enjoy living millions of lives, not just one.

Many teachers and parents don't stop and realize that when a kid with a very limited reading life walks into a library, they see a foreign language. They see spines and spines of street signs they don't know how to read, because what's the difference between science fiction and fantasy, anyway? What's the difference between action and a non-fiction book with action in it?

Where an experienced reader might know exactly the kind of spine that holds a darker story, another may not. Where they might know the difference between an older, more traditional story and a modern one, others don't. Some might say they like sports books and go to the sports section, but really, they just like that because teachers have only asked them one question: "What are you interested in?" I know that when a student says they like sports books, 99 percent of the time it is because of this. They say they like these books not because they've had great moments with them, but because it's familiar territory in an unfamiliar landscape.

We can't assume our students, especially our older students in the upper grades, know how to read the street signs of literacy. We must teach the basics. We must verbalize and model our thinking when selecting books. We must show them and guide them, no matter how old they are, or how basic of a task it is.

Nearly every student I have each year who starts by saying, "I like sports books," ends up having a far different answer later in the year. I had a group of three boys who all had this answer at the beginning of this year.

"I like sports books," they each said.

"Cool," I said. "What do you like about them?"

"I'm just into sports," each replied with a shrug.

I showed them the sports section and explored the different titles with them. We grabbed all the traditional books—the ones about star athletes and the like—and then I threw in something a little different. For every two books they were comfortable with, I'd throw in *The Crossover* by Kwame Alexander or *Ghost* by Jason Reynolds or *Gym Candy* by Carl Deuker.

Through this process these students learn what they actually like in books and what they don't. They learn they like books that deal with success and work ethic but dislike books that deal with family drama. They learn they like hearing stories about athletes, not just highlights of athletic accomplishments. They learn they like a plot, not just pure non-fiction, or they learn that some plots drag, and that they deeply want to know the statistics of their favorite athlete's glory days.

They learn.

They. Learn.

This works the other way too. I get students who read like crazy, but they only read one type of book. They read only *Harry Potter* or only fantasy or only comics. I am quick to tell these students that I have my favorite genres too, but I also push them to explore a little. They push back, and I assign a group genre study. With their group, they pick at random what genre they will study together (I make sure to put genres in the hat that most don't read often). They inevitably draw something they don't want to read or even something they *hate* (as they vehemently say).

I still give them choice in this activity. They are tasked with finding a different book within the same genre for everyone in their group. I draw some lines to guide their focus, but they still have choice.

This year I had a girl who only read *Percy Jackson* books. She was furious when she selected sports fiction as her genre. Not only did she hate sports, but she hated reading about them too. I talked with her for a long time, trying to get her in the mood to be "adventurous," but she was still angry at the whole thing.

Because I'd worked so hard to get her to trust me over the year, when I gave her *Gym Candy*, she tried it, and she fell in love with it! She had the quirkiest smile on her face when she admitted that some sports fiction could be just as good as *Percy Jackson*.

We have to be relentless in our efforts to put good books in the hands of our students. We have to let them explore. We have to build trust with them as they do so, and they'll know we will be there with the next book to help build their skill set and push them into new territories and experiences. We must meet them where they are, tell them it's okay, and be there as a helping hand rather than the arbiter of all good and acceptable literature. We must give the power of reading back to our students.

Year after year, we must guide them, watching as they stumble and soar on the road to becoming independent readers. They will create their own maps of the landscape; they don't need ours.

Lesson 15

Continuous Effort Drives Exponential Gain

Two things happened at the end of my second year of teaching.

The first and most important thing was that I started to get better.

I wasn't the best, and I didn't have it all figured out. Does anyone? I also wasn't sure how to always create engaging lessons that were as authentic as they were challenging, but I was getting comfortable in my own skin. I had worked hard during those first two years to recognize my strengths and weaknesses, which is a powerful tool for educators.

In the beginning it's easy to spin your wheels on lessons that have no place being in your classroom. I stole so many lessons from fellow teachers that simply didn't work in my space. In doing that, however, I slowly came to realize and develop my own unique style. I realized that I hate assignments that last for more than two days. Loathe would probably be a better word. I get bored. I'm a man who loves variety, but I'm also aware that some great lessons take time. After much trial and error, I started structuring my lessons in a way that felt like they were split up, although it was essentially the same lesson over a period of days. This small change allowed me to stay engaged in the learning that was occurring and keep my students engaged as well.

I make sure that I care about the lesson before I ever ask my students to care. Some argue that this is putting the educator first, but as Todd Nesloney says in his phenomenal book, *Kids Deserve It*, it's simply preserving one of the most important variables in a child's day—an excited adult.

We forget that many of our students don't actually know why or how to care about education. They haven't had an excited adult in front of them to show them the way. Every excitement they've known is based on material gain, like those found in technology or video games or some other materialistic boon. That's not necessarily bad in and of itself. For God's sake, I wrote this draft on a MacBook that is far too expensive for the little I actually do on it. I have a sixty-five-inch television, the latest game console, and a ton of other devices lying around the house. I'm not opposed to material pleasures or creature comforts, but the young people we are teaching are finding more and more value in material things. It feels less and less like they value intangibles such as loyalty, pride, discipline, and knowledge. Many of these kids don't respect the process of trial and error and have little patience for the things they aren't inherently good at doing. As with their extracurriculars and at-home amusements, it's easier to quit and move on to the next distraction than to suffer a little and get better at a hard task.

I'm part of a generation not too distanced from the one I'm discussing now, so I've seen this all firsthand. It's far too easy to fall into patterns of living that do little for us. I can't tell you how often I fight with myself to get up and work out when I know I can spend the next several hours playing video games or scrolling through social media instead. I know the struggle of overabundance. I think most of us do.

It's the fault of everyone who's ever interacted with a child for an extended period of time. We constantly show them how cool the new world of technology is but ignore the other aspects of life. When we might have taught them the value of gardening, we instead teach them the value of raising digital farms on our iPhones. When we might have taught them about the delicate balance of life on this planet, we instead teach them that if they can order something, they can have it with no apparent struggle or lasting consequences to the world at large.

My father was the adult who taught me about material gain. When he wasn't raging, sleeping, or arguing with my mom or siblings, he was buying things. He loved having the latest and greatest stuff. He'd spend thousands of dollars on stereo systems, TVs, new cars, and a bunch of small but expensive items as he desired. We ate out often, spent money as we pleased, and lived a life that was beyond our means.

In my family's early years, my father paid for all of this with the money he made through his heating and air conditioning businesses. Later, as those business began to crumble under his poor management of funds, he bought these things on credit. Then, after he paid off credit with credit until it all became too much to bear and our house was foreclosed on, his businesses finally collapsed, and we all suffered through middle-class financial ruin.

I remember the moment I finally began to see the weakness of materialism.

◇◇◇

My father had been gone for weeks at this point with the woman he briefly ran off with. My mom and I spent our days that summer digging through his belongings. All of the cabinets, safes, and sheds he kept us locked out of were finally free game. He was gone, and there were tiny secrets everywhere to find. We dug through everything. While my mom was digging away through lockboxes, I was sitting in front of his safe trying to figure out the digital combination. I eventually got it and was rewarded with rolls of quarters, some jewelry, a pill bottle, and his main pistol.

We then moved to the holy grail of locked doors—the door to his work shed. It was in here he would hide at odd hours. He'd "work" on wood projects and fix broken things around the house. With a snap, the lock broke off after my mom took a heavy-duty tool to it. The door swung open. A stale smell wafted out from the long shed.

We dug and we dug and we dug through that shed. We found more weapons, tools, odd things from work, and deep in the back, in the shadows of my father's sacred place, were ten large trash bags filled with empty pill bottles.

My mom opened them with glee at first, but that glee quickly turned to rage as she saw they were all empty.

"Your father's a sick man," she said. "Sick, sick, sick."

I stared at those bags for what felt like an hour. They represented so many of my wonderings as a child. Dots were connecting. The final illusion created by my father, the one where my mom was the sole "bad guy" in the drama of our lives, crumbled. I saw behind the curtain. I saw the puppet master's tools.

I wasn't alone. My mom discovered what would wash away her final illusions about the man she'd married: bills.

She never saw the bills because my dad controlled the cash flow and where it went. But now that her controlling husband wasn't around, she could see it all. One by one, she opened the envelopes, and one by one, they revealed she had absolutely no money to her name.

I walked in on her when this realization hit. She was on her bed, crying with a mountain of bills around her, like scattered and broken dreams.

"We're broke, Jacob!" she cried. "The bastard wasn't paying anything! He just left us to rot here."

I wanted to cry because I understood something bad had just been discovered, but I didn't understand it. Even so, I climbed on the bed and looked at all of the notices and final notes and second final notices and tried to comprehend the numbers and the statements. I told my mom it would be okay. I knew nothing.

Soon we both started digging around for anything he'd left that we could sell. My mom laid out his rifles and pistols and sold them to her friends who wanted them. We sold off his work ladders and tools, one by one. I stood by my mom as she bartered away everything she could of my father's. I was so mad with my father that I thought nothing of this. He left us—what were we supposed to do? He deserved to have everything he ever owned sold to the highest bidder. He wanted to leave us with nothing? Fine.

Of course, reality is harsh. We pocketed the cash for food and my mom used some for alcohol, and then later that week a man knocked on our door. He was young and wearing a suit. He said he had important information about our house and asked if he could come in.

I went and got my mom. She was slurring her words, and her eyes were sleepy. I eventually got her up and brought her to the living room where I had left the man.

"You're losing the house," he said.

I looked to my mom, who was blankly staring at the man in the suit.

"But," he added, "there is a way for you to make some money off of it." He then proceeded to speak at length about something I didn't understand, processes my twelve-year-old mind couldn't take in. I just sat and listened to him. I remember asking questions, which I could tell he thought odd, but since my mom wasn't responding at all, he spoke with me instead.

Eventually my mom laughed and then stood in anger. Something triggered her. She said we didn't need his help and stalked off.

The man sat in shock, shook his head, and then said goodbye to me and left.

I closed the front door and locked it, and then I heard my mom throwing things in her bedroom. I ran down the hall and stood in the doorway.

A vase left her hand and broke on the wall. The picture frames and glass decorations came next, shattering like the final pieces of our lives just had.

She was slurring and screaming and throwing.

I stood and watched and cried. I cried because I had nothing else to do. I cried because even though my mom was trying to destroy her home out of some misplaced and untamable rage, I knew it had already been destroyed.

Everything I thought I owned was about to be officially owned by someone else. All of my possessions, the home I had grown up in, and the family I thought was real had all fallen away, leaving me alone with myself.

What value was any of it if it could all be lost in an instant?

◇◇◇

I can't tell you how often, as a teacher, I've listened to adults complain about today's young people, calling them snowflakes, disrespectful, or the trophy generation. In some respects, that's fair, but it didn't happen by accident. The people who were rais-ing—and teaching—those young people helped enable their enti-tled attitudes and outlooks.

Kids do not adopt certain behaviors simply because they wake up and decide they want to be rude or selfish. They adopt these behaviors because the adults in their lives have allowed them to succeed with that behavior. We have rewarded them on some level and reinforced their decisions and wants. When a student shows a need through negative behavior, we can't reward them by giving them what they want, whether it be attention or something else. We must use the behavior to figure out what they need and work from there.

If our students or children have adopted the behavior of not caring about their academics, we shouldn't blame them for being shortsighted, disrespectful, lazy, or lost; we should be looking at ourselves and seeing what we did to reinforce their apathy. *If our children don't like to read, have we helped them understand the value in reading? Do they see us read? Do we value books over other mediums—ever?*

We subconsciously push a lot of beliefs onto the younger gen-erations. My father pushed his materialistic views on me through his actions the same way the parents of our students push their val-ues on them through their own actions. We might spout truisms about the power of reading or claim we love reading, but do they see us with books in our hands? *Do we have active reading lives? Do we model what it means to be an academic, or do we simply rule our classrooms like tyrants, pushing more and more work on them? Do we show them what it means to work hard and feel proud that we've accomplished something, or do we show them how to complain when something goes wrong?*

They say you can't expect a child to do something you don't teach, but I say you can't expect a child to do something you don't embody in your everyday actions. Our schools are filled with teachers, but how many of them are doers? Our kids watch us. They see everything. You're not hiding your annoyance as well as you think you are, and you're not inspiring an attitude for learning by avoiding the hard work of learning yourself.

There is a reason many of our leading educators are pushing for student-centered classrooms these days. We know, and the research clearly shows, that students learn best by doing. Gone are the days of lecturing and testing (and if they aren't gone where you are, they will be soon). Classrooms that put students in control and at the center of the learning succeed at higher rates, and their students are better and more roundly educated than students who do nothing but read textbooks and learn how to play the game of multiple-choice tests.

We must show students what to care about by caring about those things ourselves. If all we do is stare at our phones when we are with our students, what do we think they will come to value over time—spending time with loved ones, or looking for that next dopamine hit of social media? If we want our younger generation to read and value reading or study and value academics, we must actually read and study ourselves. We must talk about and show how reading, academics, and thinking are important parts of our lives. We must embody what it means to love books and the information inside them.

We can change our world for the better if we, the adults in the space, decide that we are all teachers, all the time. It doesn't matter if we're giving a lecture or a mini-lesson, helping a student one-on-one, or actively monitoring during a state test; we are teaching them. Our actions speak louder than our words, and you can be sure they are learning far more by watching us than they are when we are discussing the unit's vocabulary for the week.

When I started modeling not only what I wanted my students to do for their assignment but also the behaviors and attitudes I wanted them to value, my classroom increased exponentially in productivity, happiness, and quality.

I shouldn't be surprised by this, because my life has shown me this truth about modeling over and over again. When I was growing up, I always wanted to be other people. For a while, I wanted to be like my dad, then like Pudge Rodriguez of the Texas Rangers, then Neil Pert from the band Rush, then Spiderman, and then just about everyone else I admired.

Pretend was a pastime for me, and it gave me more comfort than most things. Perhaps it was my way of escaping the life I lived at home or my way of storytelling before I became a writer, but the truth is that these visions of who I could be shaped me in deep ways.

When I experienced the fall of ideals with my parents, I lost massive parts of myself. I lost foundations that were built alongside my personality, my thoughts, and my dreams.

Children watch. They see and hear everything. It's how they grow and evolve over such a short period of time. We laugh when a child shows clear signs of listening to mom or dad a little too closely by echoing a swear word, but many of us forget to see the implications of such absorption.

When I lost my parents as role models, when the illusion of them faded away like an old photograph, my mind searched for new models, new ways of operating in the world, new dreams, and new thoughts to play with and live among.

I turned to my teachers—my constants.

I watched them like a hawk, like all kids do, and I learned about the possibilities outside of my home.

If this book is anything, it's proof of great teachers making an impact by simply modeling a better life. By being kind, they model a world in which smiles, good manners, and relentless support are normal. By being disciplined, they model a world in which we don't just mindlessly consume everything in sight but consciously choose where to concentrate our efforts. By being passionate, they model a world in which it's okay to dream big and reach for those damn stars above us.

The wonderful teachers I had, the ones mentioned in this book and the ones who aren't, did this for me. As a kid who saw drug addiction after drug addiction, issue after issue, and fight after fight, adults who functioned without those hang-ups were like cool drinks of water to my mouth that had gone dry after a night of yelling.

How much value did they bring by just being there? How many times did they show up with any number of personal problems going on and still do their job for us kids in class? They might not have hidden their own stress all the time, but what I remember is how they treated me when I was in their class, not the few bad days they had during a given school year.

The second thing that happened to me at the end of my second year of teaching was that I was able to focus on improvement. I had reached a point where I wasn't simply trying to survive; I was beginning to thrive. I had time to reflect on my practices as I attempted to refine, discard, and evolve to create a classroom that was next-level to everything I'd done thus far.

I wanted to grow more, and I wanted to learn from the people who were at the top of their games. Rather than going up to each individual educator I admired or followed on social media and asking for advice, I came up with an idea that would not only help me but also thousands of educators around the world.

— Lesson 16 —

Energy Is Infectious

One day I was sitting in a campus staff meeting in our school library. I watched as teachers filed in one by one and two by two. Some were laughing, others had a disheveled look about them, and many just came in and went about their business, surely wondering how long the meeting would be.

The meeting started. We were going over this or that. I don't really remember, to be honest. But eventually, some teachers began demonstrating a lesson they had created. They were modeling a structure they found useful while giving us details we needed about campus news. I remember analyzing it, watching their moves, seeing if it was something I could use in my classroom. They incorporated movement and discussion. They modeled moving around the room and taking brief assessments of the learning that was happening by asking individual groups targeted questions.

And then it was over. We all clapped and gave them the praise they deserved, and then we moved back into the style of staff meeting too many of us are familiar with.

I remember thinking that the good part of the meeting, the part that actually taught me something, was over too soon, and then we spent too long on the other parts, the parts these meetings are known for—sit and get and grow weary.

I found myself wanting a way to talk to my colleagues more. Many of them had been teaching for longer than me and, because of that, had ideas that just didn't occur to me.

The issue was, everyone was busy. I would get caught up in something and not make it to their classrooms to talk about or watch a lesson. They'd get caught up and feel anxious if I grilled them about what they were doing too often. And in the end, we'd both be barely better off than after the short staff meeting demonstration.

But what if there was a reason for us to talk, to explore, to examine best practices and the way we experience them? What if there was a forum that allowed us to come together and truly have an honest discussion about our teaching lives and everything that entails?

I'd podcasted before and listened to several, and once I had the idea to create a reason for discussion, I knew it was a great fit for this idea. Nothing fancy—just a mic, a computer, and two teachers discussing whatever was on their minds at the time.

A few days later, I approached my principal, past teacher, and good friend, James Whitfield, about the idea. I think the pitch went something like this:

"Hey, Whitfield, I have an idea."

His eyes lit up a little, as he was always game for anything new. "What is it?"

"I was thinking. We have a lot of great teachers on campus, and some of them I never get to talk to or see. What if we had a podcast where I interviewed our teachers here? Nothing big, just something that we could all listen to and get ideas from."

He was nodding along by this point, and I could see the gears in his mind turning. "You know, I like that."

The idea, in truth, was just a digital, ongoing, campus Professional Learning Community (PLC). Every week I would interview a teacher, discuss a topic of choice in a conversational tone, and then release it on the website for the podcast and podcasting services like iTunes so people could download it easily.

Boom. The *Teach Me, Teacher* podcast was born.

I didn't know how to track podcast downloads at the time, so when I started, and for several months after that, I had no idea if anyone was really listening. I assumed some were—probably the few teachers at the school who liked the Facebook page I made for *Teach Me, Teacher*. But other than that, I wasn't sure.

A few months later, after I figured out how to track podcast downloads and traffic, I was shocked to see that I was getting a few hundred downloads a month from across the world.

To be honest, I didn't know what to think! My little project, designed to connect the teachers at my school, was somehow reaching others in the United States and around the world. I hadn't meant for this to happen and hadn't advertised or posted much about it on social media. I was just recording conversations with the educators I looked up to and who I thought had something valuable to say about teaching or education.

Knowing that many others were listening began to change how I approached the podcast. Slowly, especially as thousands more started listening, I cultivated the podcast into what it has become today: a continual conversation between teachers meant to help other teachers. Although the show has had bigger and bigger guests, the DNA of the show remains focused on spotlighting teachers and the craft of teaching.

The Facebook page grew to include thousands of educators. I started making videos. The show had a constant spot on iTunes' top education charts. My network of educators grew, and thus my reach and my ability to explore alongside others and delve into the best and brightest information grew as well. Tens of thousands of listeners from more than eighty countries tune in every month to hear educators discuss their practices.

Teach Me, Teacher became something huge, and it all started with the desire to talk, listen, and learn.

I believe the success of the podcast is due to the energy of the show.

Energy is infectious. We're all so tired of the same old, same old that when we see something new and exciting, we reach out and cling to it. Every day is filled with obstacles and reasons to quit trying, so when we find something that reminds us of the beauty and wonder of life, we return to it to get refueled for the work ahead of us.

Thanks to fabulous guests—from veteran teachers to major thought leaders to young practitioners—we've created a show that is a positive force in the educational community. By ensuring that every show is filled with laughter, honesty, and insight, we've created something teachers can trust and believe in.

I say frequently on the podcast that the show was shaped entirely by the educators who came and listened and then shared it with others. No question about it. I've spent very few of my own dollars spreading the word about the show and definitely not enough to garner thousands of listeners all over the world.

I'm proud that I was able to help build something that is beneficial to educators across the globe, but I'm proudest of continuing to give educators a reason to keep learning and evolving. If I can give one educator somewhere hope in their role, I consider my work a success. If my stories here in this book can inspire one teacher to push on and be reignited to keep giving their all to their students, I am content.

Teach Me, Teacher is a small example of the revolution in education. It isn't me, and it isn't an individual guest; it is a collective revolutionary mindset that's driving great practices and philosophies in schools everywhere. Teachers are sharing more than ever thanks to the power of social media and a willingness to record the magic of our classrooms. More and more teachers are starting to pay attention. Outsiders are slowly seeing what real educators are doing in schools, not the caricatures that politicians and idle social gossipers hold up as reality.

Teach Me, Teacher continues to remind me that education is on the rise. More and more teachers are embracing the new and exciting world of "teacher as the rock star," and rightly so. We even have our own teacher celebrities now: Ron Clark, Kim Bearden, Hope and Wade King, Dave Burgess, Adam Dovico, Todd Nesloney, Penny Kittle, Kelly Gallagher, Donalyn Miller, Jeff Anderson, Josie Bensko, Kelli Sanders, Halee Sikorski, Joe Dombrowski (Mr. D), Esther Brunat, Haley Curfman, Brittany Sinitch, Marie Morris, Megan Forbes, Colby Sharp, Danny Steele, Todd Whitaker, Mary Howard, Evan and Laura Robb, Amy Fast, Shae Saeed, and many, many others. There's an astounding number of educators I didn't list those who have built their audiences by sharing the cool things they are doing on Instagram and Twitter.

If this isn't the golden age to be a teacher, then it's the stage just before the golden age. We've never had so much positivity, such easy access to amazing lessons shared by brilliant educators, and so many ways to build our digital learning communities beyond our school walls. Twitter chats, Instagram follow threads, and a constant stream of posts and videos are all testimonies of the brilliant things happening in education.

For all of the optimism, there is a lot of doom and gloom regarding education these days. News broadcasts and certain corners of social media take turns trashing on education and teachers.

To that I say . . .

If you don't believe in education's future, you're not paying attention.

Energy feeds energy. I'm just glad that *Teach Me, Teacher* continues to thrive among and with so much greatness out there.

Doubt Is a Tool
for Reflection

I spent a lot of time watching home videos as a kid. I loved them. I think it was my way of seeing my family in a different light. The older the video, the fewer fights we had, and the less rot there was in their souls.

I remember a lot about my family through these videos. Large pieces of my recollection are gone, blocked off by events worth forgetting, but the videos remain clear to me. They allow me to experience a little of the world into which I was born. They allow me to peer into the beginnings, before it all became irreversibly toxic.

There is a pair of videotapes buried in a box somewhere that show my father playing drums with an old friend and guitarist out at the lake. It starts outside in the summer heat. The ground is a light brown, with gravel paving the path up to a shack. Cars are parked. Kids are running around. The sound of 1970s and 1980s style rock-n-roll is shaking and moving in the distance, just up a small hill.

As the camera gets closer, the music gets louder, and you see everyone gathered around the red Ludwig altar and my dad on the throne inside it.

The spectators have beers, and they're laughing and dancing. The guitarist is feeling the audience, smiling back and giving them what they want. My father is in the zone, a cigarette dangling in his mouth, living out the final moments of a failed dream.

I'm about three, and I'm in front of his red drum set with sticks in my hand, shaking my head side to side in rhythm with the music.

There I was, in front of my father's drum set, and there I will be for years. This image of light blond Jacob, sticks in hand, watching his dad religiously, is such a pure and telling scene. I'm watching the way he plays, learning the feel, the beat, and the tempo. I'm becoming a musician song by song. I'm becoming a performer.

Like every kid, I took in the models in front of me.

As I was able to catch more of what he was doing rhythmically in his performance, I began to take it and make it my own. I believe that my need and desire to perform, be on stage, and provide energy to the people around me when I'm at the center of attention stems from my obsession with these videos.

My father liked to be at the center of attention. He was a host. He was an entertainer. He was the center of his circle of friends back when they would still come around. Our childhood birthdays, documented by our family's video cameras, were just excuses for my parents to party. They would do the presents and the birthday cake, and then they would turn up the Metallica or AC/DC, drink beer, and laugh the night away.

I'm nostalgic about very little, but this is something I miss because they were the moments I loved as a kid.

Years later, when my dad's skills as a drummer began to falter, I took over. When we had parties, I was the one who played. We would go to the garage, and everyone would party around me while I performed.

This exposure to performance was a high unlike any other and one that I've loved ever since. This is the basic drive that inspires me to give my students experiences they won't forget. It also drives me to participate in dance-offs at pep-rallies when someone feels like they can take me on.

This exposure to performance drives me to want to write a great book for you and create internet content that not only inspires and informs educators but also entertains.

While growing up, I never really doubted myself. I had a lot of confidence built up over years of being the center of attention in my home. I was also competent in a lot of what I did and took to new skills easily.

All of this equaled out eventually, and I learned that a lot of people are good at a lot of things. When I was young and my circle was small, I stood out. As I got older, I stood out less. I imagine this is the natural course of things. If it wasn't, then everyone would be rock stars, movie stars, and professional athletes. Most of us have to eventually realize we aren't as good as we think we are. We aren't in the 1 percent that makes it big in these extremely competitive fields.

The biggest revelation I had was about my ability as a drummer. It was the skill I had stuck with the longest and the one most deeply rooted in my soul. Music was my religion before I ever even tried to look up.

I just knew I would make it as a musician. I would be a famous drummer or, at the very least, make a living playing music. The band I formed with my cousin in my teenage years was bound to make it big. We had recordings, great tunes, and a passion for what we played.

I don't know when it happened, but at a certain point I realized I wasn't that good. I had talent, as my drum director had told me, yet I lacked essential control. I sounded good to people who didn't know better, but when I would go back and listen to my work, I was off time in parts or, worse, inaccurate in my rhythms. I was what you would call an amateur. I could please a small crowd, but I wasn't anything special. I didn't have what it takes to reach the next level or the drive to make it happen.

It's possible that with enough practice I could have tightened up my craft. I could have worked on my timing, labored on my rhythms, and evolved to become something special. A part of me still thinks being a professional drummer is a viable option for my life, but I know it isn't.

I changed. When I was seventeen, I found a girl I loved, married her, and had a son. I later fell in love with teaching and education and built a different life from the one I dreamed about as a kid.

I should say I never felt that getting married or having a child of my own held me back from music. My father did, and that's why he hated me watching videos of the musician he used to be. He'd chosen to be the cliché musician who couldn't live his dreams because of his life choices. He failed to see how amazing it is to build a family and a life. I've learned from his missteps.

On some level I knew music wasn't going to be where I went with my life, especially as I got older and the real world demanded my attention. I still played, wrote songs, and jammed the way I always did, but I realized I was meant to do other things.

I can't help but wonder if the doubts got to me early, though. Did I change, or did reality slowly insert more doubts into my mind, causing me to lose hope in doing something very few people get to do? It's a chicken-or-the-egg argument in a lot of ways.

For the longest time, I had zero doubts. I was blindly confident in my abilities in anything I tried. I attribute this cockiness to my father. He was a brutal, cruel, and abusive human being, and he was also extremely confident in himself, at least outwardly. Abusive people, by nature, have holes in their confidence. Why else would they feel the need to control others? I'm sure if we dove into the elements that made up his psyche, we'd find all sorts of inferiority complexes. As a child I didn't know this. I just knew what I saw, which was a man who laughed a lot, was the center of parties, and was praised for his drumming abilities.

For a long time, I idolized my father. I have a clear memory of sitting at the dinner table with my family and telling my parents that I wanted to be just like dad. He laughed his smokers laugh as I listed off all of his traits I wanted to emulate.

It took a few years, but my aspirations changed. I saw through my father's outward appearance. I saw the darkness in his mind.

I started to doubt.

I had always believed my family had a lot of money, but as the fights about financial issues increased, I began to doubt.

I believed my father was a successful businessman, and then I saw how often he changed his business' name and how often he and my mom talked about screwing over customers for a few extra dollars. My mom once told me how he "would always say he needed to do something extra at a job site when fixing someone's air conditioner and get them to pay him in cash."

I believed that my father was proud of me as a drummer, and then I realized he was just living through me. He never made it as a musician, so he wanted to live that dream through me.

Although I haven't talked to him in years, I can't help but wonder if he regrets never seeing me at my best and brightest as a drummer.

Perhaps this happens to most of us. We grow up idolizing our parents, and then as we grow older, the magic wears off and we see them for what they are: human. In my case, they were humans who made far too many poor choices. In other cases, they are humans who make mistakes but are good in spite of those. I'm sure my parents have good in them still, but it shows so little these days, and it's hard to discuss here.

Now in my late twenties, I can't help but reflect daily on doubt. I feel it so much more than when I was young. The realities of life have set in over the years, and doubt is around every corner.

As I type, I find myself doubting my ability to write this book—this chapter—this sentence. I doubt if people will care about this work, if I'm wasting my time, if I can reach my daily word goals, if I can write honestly, if people will care about my life and how it has informed my teaching beliefs and practices, if, if, if . . .

I'll doubt my lesson plans. When my students begin working on their group genre study projects, where students self-select books within a genre to learn about it, I'll doubt if this new idea for my class will work. Will they learn? Will they grow as readers and thinkers?

I'll doubt spending so much time letting my kids read, despite knowing that the research overwhelmingly demonstrates the benefits of this practice. I'll doubt, because they should be *doing* something, right? They should be working! Funny that, even as an ELA teacher who believes in the power of independent reading, I still sometimes slip into old ways of thinking. Doubts do that; they drag us backwards.

I'll doubt my ability to teach a lesson.

I'll doubt my podcast and its power to help teachers all around the world.

I'll doubt that teaching is truly my passion.

What if I'm supposed to be a fiction author? Or a business-man? Or any number of other things? I'm young. What makes me believe this is where I'm supposed to be? Who the hell am I to feel as if I've figured something out about myself?

In a slightly serious way, I'm skeptical of people who are extremely confident in themselves. I knew I wanted to be a teacher back in high school (in a roundabout way), but that wasn't enough to erase doubts. I doubted myself all the way into a degree that wasn't in teaching and a job that I hated.

I see confident people everywhere and ask how they are so sure in their choices. Did they always know they wanted to be teachers? Did they ever have any doubts? Did they always know they wanted to go into sales? Did they always know they wanted to work with computers? Be chefs? Design houses?

What astounds me even more is when people are confident in their beliefs. Beliefs are fluid in my world. My childhood faith died, was replaced by a staunch atheism, and then evolved into something that resembles, at best, a hodgepodge of ideas and belief structures, abandoned and secured at will. I could go to sleep thinking deeply about the gospels, wake up with my mind on the Atman and Brahman, and then by lunch be contemplating *The Hero with a Thousand Faces* by Joseph Campbell and what it could possibly mean on a spiritual level for the human species.

I doubt everything. When my beliefs about my family burned to ash, so did my faith in anything. Doubt continues to permeate my life. I reflect on this doubt, and though it feels a bit like walking on thin ice, it's this reflection that drives me further.

I doubt.

And yet . . .

Hope

I hope.

My hope is fueled by my doubts. I replaced my inherited cockiness, over time, with something much stronger and more resilient. Rather than believing everything I touch will turn to gold, I *hope* it will. I see the possibility. I doubt, and yet I use those doubts to drive my purpose and vision.

I hope my ability as a teacher will help me reach and inspire more and more kids to find their passions in life and pursue them relentlessly.

I hope my lessons get students to engage in the learning and produce authentic work.

I hope my students will not only read more every week but also enjoy it more every week. Reading promotes compassion and lowers the stress of the reader, and I hope I see this with every student in my class.

I hope I keep my passion for teaching alive, that you will too, and that we will all continue being the difference-makers to so many students across the world.

Everything I've accomplished as an educator and individual is due to my hope being louder than my doubt. Where my doubt nags, my hope sings. Where my doubt crawls, my hope soars.

I try to use the life-giving energy of hope to make a positive difference. I think you have to if you have goals that are big. Confidence can help drive your actions, but it takes big hope to do big things.

Confidence will help you start your book, but hope in your vision and message fuels you when the book writing becomes tough.

Confidence will help you start a YouTube channel or Instagram account to share your teaching ideas, but hope that good will come for you and others from sharing your stories will keep you posting long after the novelty has worn off.

Confidence will help you try something new in the classroom, but hope in the power of a great lesson, class, and school will push you to try even more things.

You do it because you believe in yourself and you have hope for the future.

Let's not waste our time pretending. Hope is underrated. The "realists" out there will give us a thousand reasons not to hope and will back those reasons up with logic and evidence. We are products of our environment to a large degree, and the people around us help shape us for our successes and failures. Be humble and listen to others around you, but don't let their doubt strangle the power in your hope.

I know several people who want to get out there and show their work to people, but they are frozen by a fear of judgment and controlled by their doubt and the doubts of others.

You have to have big hopes to dream big. You have to let that hope fill you up to put your work out there, especially when you're surrounded by people who would rather see you succumb to doubt and live a lesser, caged life.

When I started the *Teach Me, Teacher* podcast, I did so with one goal in mind: to bring together the many ideas floating around my school. Teachers learn best from other teachers, and there were some exceptional educators in our building that we never heard from. I wanted to give those folks a voice.

As it turned out, other people wanted to learn from them too, and the podcast grew, attracting listeners from across the world. Educators began telling me that the show helped them remember why they became a teacher. My hope swelled with every compliment, every iTunes review, and every new record number of monthly downloads.

Today, as I book bigger names on the show, I sometimes doubt my ability to capitalize on the opportunity that has grown from this experiment. In the end, however, my hope wins out, and I am reminded that I have a chance to influence teachers around the world and help guide and renew their passions for this beautiful profession. I have a chance to encourage teachers to allow their kids to *read* in reading class. I have a chance to encourage teachers to teach, not just run through the motions. I have a chance to help educators remember their *why* before it's too late.

I don't do any of this because I believe that I'm the savior of education or that my podcast will revolutionize the world; I do it because I have hope in the power of sharing. Would I love to see my show at the top of the podcast charts? Of course. Do I hope this will happen? Absolutely. I also hope that the show helps people, that it encourages and uplifts even just one educator. Some of my hope drives my ambition, and some of it drives the grind. It's not enough to have big dreams and goals. If it were, we'd all be famous. We have to be willing to put in the effort as well.

We must also have hope for those goals that are less about us and more about whom we help.

We can hope to be the teachers with the best scores, but we must also hope for our struggling students to make significant gains.

We can hope our students will read fifty books each, but we must also hope that our challenged readers will find one amazing book that changes their lives.

We can hope for the grand stuff to happen, but we must also realize the road to success is paved by the work we do day in and day out. You create a great piece of art one stroke at a time.

I'm not sure where my hope came from. No one ever told me about the power of hope. I didn't read about it in a book or learn about it on YouTube. I think I just found it, like a small piece of treasure lost in the mountains. Perhaps I found it in watching my home movies. In seeing what my family was, maybe I developed hope that we could be like that again. Maybe my hope, like so many things, came to me as a gift from a place I don't fully understand.

If you haven't found the power of hope or if you've lost it along the way, perhaps I can be the one that gives it to you.

Know this: hope is good. Hope is resilient. Hope is powerful. Hope is louder than doubt.

Let yourself hope, and then turn around and encourage your students to hope. Allow them to dream.

What a shame it is to see teachers and parents quash the fantasies of a child. Childhood is beautiful in its wonder and imagination. One of the greatest teachers of all time didn't tell us to be like children because he wanted us to be simple; he told us to be like children because of how immensely liberated their minds can be. We are born into this world free. It's only as we get older that bars are added to our surroundings, these cages built by circumstances, and we begin to lose our dreams.

When we lose or fail—and when our students lose or fail— we must model hope. As Martin Luther King, Jr. said, "We must accept finite disappointment but never lose infinite hope."

— Lesson 19 —

Find the Kids Who Hide

When I was young, I dreaded being picked up from my elementary school. I would sit outside, sometimes waiting for an hour or longer, wondering who would take me home.

Would it be the mom I loved? The mom who had a sense of humor. The one my friends thought was the "cool mom."

Or would it be the slurring mom? The mom whose eyes were vague pools, murky windows into her doped-up mind. The one who would tell us she was tired, her tongue and hands and head moving slowly. The one who swerved on the road, nearly hitting cars as my sister and I screamed to keep her awake.

Or would it be the angry mom? The one who shoved her foot on the gas pedal in anger and scared the living hell out of me as we flew down streets, then slammed on the brakes so that the seat belt dug into my skin. The one who took out her frustrations on her kids, who smacked us if we talked back, and who continued the fight once we got home.

One day in particular, it was the angry mom who arrived to take me home.

I'd been waiting for a while outside my school. All of my friends were gone, and most of the adults had left as well. Standing in the grass, I was busy investigating all the trees and bushes. I always liked to explore, pretending that I was discovering something or walking into a place few people had walked before. I pretended a lot.

When my mom showed up, I was glad to be leaving. It was hot, and I was sweating. As soon as I opened the door to the Suburban, I knew which mom I was dealing with. She was mad at something—I don't remember what it was. She was also slurring a bit.

My gut tightened. My tongue scratched itself on my teeth, as if doing so would make anything better.

I remember being mad at her as I flung my backpack inside, and we had already started to argue, perhaps about her being late, as I put my foot in the car. Without any warning, fueled by anger and pills, she stepped on the gas and took off down the street. With one leg in the car and one leg out, I flew back and landed on the concrete. The passenger door of the car flung open as I watched her take off down the street without me.

Shock ran through my body. I wanted to cry and yell and storm in anger and do nothing, all at once. But I just sat there, in complete disbelief. Little did I know I would be thrown off another SUV by my mom on a summer night several years later.

She eventually realized I wasn't in the car and came back to pick me up.

Maybe she apologized. Maybe she blamed me. Maybe we fought more, or maybe I was silently angry. I don't know. This moment has blurred over the years. I remember falling to the concrete outside of my school, but beyond that my memory of that day is just a haze of anger and fear.

That's the thing with these types of memories. I know the highlights. I feel my school's sidewalk on my lower back. I feel the anger brewing behind my eyes as I sat there and watched the car drive off. I feel the overwhelming truth of it all coursing through my veins like fire.

It's the silent movie of abuse, the wordless picture book drawn by a child's emotions that are fine-tuned enough to make sense of it all. It's a fire that burns over decades.

This fire was kindled when I was a kid, and it continued to grow until I was an adult. So much anger comes with a family like mine. So much fear, anxiety, and white-hot rage exist when you live with parents who will throw you off of a car, endanger your life by driving on the highway when they're high, and torture you with abuse, both physical and mental.

This anger came out in my writing as a kid. I loved when we had time to write in school. It gave me an out, much like my music did. I would write stories about boys fighting off demons in their house or about surviving murderers and monsters in my home. It was dark for a kid in elementary school, but it was how my pain came out.

And do you know what? My teachers used this to help me. They met me where I was and allowed my creativity to foster in my art. I don't ever remember them once forcing me to change the content I wrote about, some of which was quite dark. Instead, they encouraged me and developed my skills through my choices.

My fourth-grade teacher, Mrs. Urban, loved to read our stories aloud to the class. She would have us all gather in a circle, and we would wait eagerly to see if our story would be selected.

When she chose a story of ours to read, she always focused on the writing or the style. She complimented the way we used continuous sounds to show the passage of time or the creativity of our descriptions. She would point out what we did well and encourage the good writing decisions we made.

She could have easily not read my stories because of their dark nature, but she chose to use them to highlight the good in my work. She took what I gave her and found the gold in it.

This high from being rewarded with praise continued to inspire me to write, and I wrote a lot in fifth grade as well. My writing became darker, and my skill improved, because Mr. Hansen gave me constructive feedback on how to show intentions in characters. He asked me to explain more, to think about why the murderer was attacking the boy, and to show rather than tell.

They met me where I was so I could improve on the pieces that mattered most to my academics, all without me knowing. They could have made it an official lesson, but instead, they made me believe they loved my writing and wanted more of it. I didn't know they were slowly training me in a craft that would serve me for years to come.

As a teacher today, I am constantly asking questions that stem from my own childhood experience. How many of our students are living through childhoods like mine? How many of our kids are afraid to get in the car when they leave school? Which ones are wondering which mom will show up? Which ones wait for more than an hour to be picked up, only to suffer once they are?

Many of them hide, as I did.

I didn't wear this anxiety on my sleeve in school. Once I was in those doors, I was "school Jacob." I was filled with energy, played games in gym class, and achieved at fairly high levels (until high school, at least). School was a place where I could forget about my mom and dad for a while. When you grow up in a house of abuse, violence, and drugs, it's normal to hide it from the rest of the world. I didn't consciously choose to hide it. I wasn't aware that I was hiding it. I just did it.

There were signs of what I was going through. Some of it leaked into my creative writing, just as my students' lives do now in theirs.

Every week my students turn in a one-page reflection of their choosing that they take through the writing process. Sometimes I put restrictions on what they write, such as format (essay, poem, narrative), and sometimes I'll give them a topic, but I often just let them write whatever they'd like in the hopes of empowering and cultivating their ability to choose what to work on.

I love these papers. Getting to read the writing of my students tells me so much about them. I learn about their world, their thought processes, and their hopes and dreams—what they'll share, at least.

Sometimes I see the familiar signs of dysfunction. They'll write about fights they have with their family or how they feel mistreated or misunderstood. They'll write about how they can't wait for dad or mom to get out of jail so they don't have to live with grandma anymore. Or they'll write stories about family members on drugs or about violence in the home. Some show a tendency to the darker side of art, and some only talk about the entertainment they enjoy (both reveal a lot about their home lives).

Maybe I acted out sometimes in school, like some of my students do. I wasn't ever in trouble, but I wasn't afraid to make comments in class to try to get a laugh from my peers. Many of my students are like this as well.

I had a student who was brighter than the sun and got in trouble more times a week than hours I would sleep. We had a rough start to the beginning of our time together. He was in my detention halls weekly and quickly requested to get out of my Pre-AP classes.

This kid had all of the natural intelligence he needed to grow in life, but certain behaviors stopped him from achieving at higher levels. He could write beautifully with keen insights, but it would take him twenty minutes just to get focused. He'd complain about having to do the work and then constantly need affirmations once he started working.

Once he understood that I was only executing the consequences of his behaviors because I cared about him, I was able to dive deeper into his needs and see a glimmer of why he acted the way he did.

In that student I saw a kid who had a lack of validation in his life. His priority was sports, and he regularly tried to find ways not to read in my class. He was a young man who loved distraction, not focus. He wanted to be the center of attention in class as long as we weren't discussing anything intellectual.

I started to show him how smart he was simply by getting him to use his brains for actual content-based objectives with peers who would appreciate him. In a few weeks, he started to show more willingness to do the hard work of thinking and learning.

He still craved validation, but now he sought it out more for his thoughts and less for his quips. And while he still occasionally groaned at the thought of reading a book, he smiled when I gave him my teacher glare, and then he got to reading.

Student behaviors show a need. In the end it doesn't always matter why children do what they do; it matters that we do something to help them.

When the quiet of reading falls on my classroom, I often wonder what my wonderful students are hiding inside their heads. *What kind of home life do they leave behind each morning? What role does school truly play in their lives? What kinds of emotions do they experience when they know it's time to leave school each day?*

Some wear their emotions right on their faces and shoulders, but many don't. Many hide so well that we don't ever pause to wonder what their struggles are, if they're afraid to go home, or if they even have a home to go to at all.

How do we reach out to them? How do we let them know that they're seen, loved, and cared for? How do we make sure that none of our students hide so much and so well that they disappear altogether?

Do What's Right for Your Students

I fundamentally believe that responding to our students' needs trumps any district, campus, or personal initiative we are currently pursuing.

The worst cases I've ever seen of teachers making bad decisions for their students, myself included, are the result of a fear of rebelling against initiatives and mandates. No one wants to get in trouble, get a bad evaluation, or fear for their job, but one thing I've learned during my time as an educator—and after talking to some of the best minds in education on *Teach Me, Teacher*—is that no initiative is all encompassing. It is absolutely absurd to operate on the assumption that any one idea, or combination of a few ideas (often called an "action plan"), is able to guide teachers in every situation that comes up in our classrooms. Despite that reality, many teachers make decisions based on something other than their students.

I hear it when I talk to teachers off the air on the podcast. I hear it when I'm at a training and listen to teachers talk about why they can't implement what they're learning because of their principal or district, even though the principal or district sent them to the training. I see it in various teacher groups on Facebook or scrolling through the comments on an education-focused video.

Good teachers do what is asked of them and support their students. Great teachers support their students, regardless of what is asked by the powers that be.

I don't believe districts, principals, or anyone making decisions about what teachers should do in their classrooms are actively trying to hurt kids or their education, but I do think people who are disconnected from the classrooms can make decisions that don't support young people in the best possible way.

I get it. Schools need action plans and goals, and districts must always be looking at improvement, because at the end of the day, those administrators' jobs are on the line, and if they screw up too much, then schools and teachers' jobs could be on the line too. But there has to be a better way—a more rational and humane way—of allowing teachers to teach not just the curriculum but the whole child as well.

Our students' needs are greater than standards and test scores, especially in high-poverty schools where standards and test scores are stressed even more. It's a shame that students with statistically lower levels of achievement, lower household income, and less access to books and other materials that will set them up for a good education before they ever come into a classroom get forced into drill-and-kill lessons because of the population they are a part of. We take kids who need the most engaging, inspiring, and rigorous lessons, and we force-feed them a diet of programs and worksheets and shove them into weekend state-testing tutorials, all so we can say we made gains of a few percentage points on a standardized test.

This issue becomes even more apparent in reading intervention, where we take the kids who need the most guidance and exposure to great books and sit them in front of computer programs. We make it extremely difficult for them to love reading by forcing them to track their Lexile and answer endless multiple-choice questions.

I've met many teachers who are forced to teach with programs or use tools such as Accelerated Reader when they know it's not inspiring students to be readers. While these programs do wonders to gamify reading, the supporters of such an outcome never stop to ask if gamifyng reading is a good way to create a literate society. Some districts are led to believe these "remedial" programs will raise scores in a meaningful way. Others believe the hype presented in corporate propaganda and the self-conducted "research" sold to educators in slick presentations.

When people insult public education, they are imagining classrooms where computer programs and digital worksheets pass as best practices to support struggling students.

I don't blame people for insulting this method of teaching.

Struggling kids need more than digital programs to inspire them to overcome their obstacles. They need caring and supportive adults to look into their eyes and tell them they've got this. They need teachers to high five them when they succeed and pick them up when they fall.

In my third year of teaching, I began to embody this vision. I was proficient in my craft at this point, so I was finally able to focus on these details and aspects of my job. My work became less about what I had to do and more about what I needed to do.

I started asking the important questions: What does this period need? What does this student or group need? What do my students need emotionally? What do my students need intellectually? What do my students need from me or from this class? What's best for my classes right now, in this moment?

That was the year teaching evolved to a higher level. I became a responsive teacher. In essence, I started caring less about what I had planned or needed to do and more about what my students needed from me in the moment.

Teachers have so much content to get through in the course of a school year. Our curricula are tight, and some of us have scripts that need to be followed to the letter. But our work is deeper than a script. Too many people think our purpose in the classroom is to make sure we hit arbitrary markers of progress. District mandates certainly assume this from time to time.

That approach simply doesn't interest me, and I have no use for it.

I look at my students, and I ask myself what I need to be for them at that moment. The lives, minds, and souls of our children are greater than any date on a calendar or piece of curriculum we must check off a list by the end of the week.

I am a stronger educator today because I make the choice to place my students' needs ahead of all the mandates and action plans. That doesn't mean I ignore the direction of my district and its administrators. Most of their decisions are made with positive intentions and with kids in mind. At the same time, life happens. Our kids come in with new and different needs every day. Dates, schedules, and curriculum standards are important and can serve as helpful guides, but my students take precedence every single time and without waiver.

What good does it do to move on to the second unit when I know my kids aren't getting the first unit? What good does it do to force more work down kids' throats when they are struggling to finish the work I've already assigned? What good does it do to ignore learning gaps and plow ahead to the next marker simply because someone somewhere said I had to?

The answer is clear to me.

When Mrs. Urban sat me down in the back of the room and gave me tools to handle my home life, she was responding to my needs. How many other times did she teach me in the moment that I can't remember? How many other teachers did I have who taught me what I needed—what my entire class needed—because it was the right thing to do, and faced the consequences later? How often did they get behind because they saw a need and responded to it? Based on my own classroom experience and watching great teachers in schools across the world, I would guess it's more than we think.

Teaching requires courage to stand up and do what's right for kids. Doing what's right for the kids will always epitomize superior teaching.

— Lesson 21 —

Suffering Produces Endurance

My mom was an abused woman. She lived with and loved men who treated her terribly. She felt their fists and their hateful words. She took the poisons they fed her and the ones she willingly asked for.

If you've read this far, you know I haven't held back my feelings about my mother. I feel like I owe you, the reader, that much in a memoir. I don't blame her for everything, yet I don't blame others for her choices. I wasn't there for every decision she made, but I was there for twenty years of them. I've seen with my own eyes the struggle she's had to fight through, and I've seen her willingly stay in the struggle. I've seen her feel as guilty and as remorseful as possible for lying to me and then turn around and do it again and again and again.

I don't look at her with hate, but I do look with anger.

I'm angry she's never made it out. I'm angry at the choices she's made and the actions she's taken. I'm angry that the world has dealt her the cards it has. I'm angry I can only do so much to help her. I'm angry that I've been put in situations by her actions, her words, and her hands, many of which I haven't included in this book. I can't even describe them. Most of all, I'm angry that as I started to push out and break free from our family's hell, her disdain and vitriol towards me rose to a fever pitch.

When you live around people who suffer as if it's all there is, you hurt them the most when you try to break free, and the only way they think they'll feel better is if they hold you down, hope for your failure, or actively try to break you down until you quit. They want you to come back to their world of suffering.

People on the outside who see you growing will do this too. The moment you begin to push against the grain to get to the next level, people who are failing or who are trapped in their own existences will wish upon every star for you to fail. People who willingly suffer do not like to see others try to break the cycle.

It is a truth I've learned through my family experiences, but I've seen it echoed many times since, especially in my professional practice as a young man who's hungry to make a difference and a positive mark on the world.

When I turned eighteen, I got a job working at Walgreens and met the girl I would later move in with and marry. Once I was old enough, I started to see opportunities for freedom. I started to see the world outside. Almost as soon as I saw them, I pursued them, and those then made new opportunities.

All the years of suffering were losing their grip on my mind. They were clawing to stay, oh yes they were, but I was breaking away, one step at a time.

By the time I was twenty, I had been in school for a few years earning my degree, and I was getting married. I changed jobs,

made more money, and evolved. I began to grow up. I had a son and became a father. My wife and I became closer, better, and stronger. My world began to take shape, and the pain and suffering of my childhood faded into the distance with a whimper.

And then a phone call would come from my mom. She would be angry at me for avoiding her calls, which I did often. She'd leave me messages about the latest problems of the family. She would tell me how she was finally done with my sister who still couldn't hold a job and support her kids, how she was over the drama, or how I shouldn't believe what I'm hearing about the fight that happened over the weekend. Any number of things. The same song and dance, repeatedly and without fail.

And then the phone calls would become irate. She'd yell at me, calling me names I won't immortalize here. She'd say that I was no longer her son and that I was the most worthless person she'd ever met. Days later, or even hours later, she'd heavily slur an apology and pretend like things were normal again, the cycle of suffering on clear display.

With every step I took to move away from the life I grew up in, something or someone would try to pull me back.

Suffering people don't want others to be happy. It's why their relationships rot from the inside out. It's why the most unhappy people attract other unhappy people. They feed off one another. They also feed on the demise of those trying to make things better or escape the cycle of suffering.

Above all else, this is why I didn't and still can't return to my family. By the time I was a teacher, I had all but severed my ties to my family (with the exception of my oldest brother). I had to. To be the father my child needed, to be the husband my wife deserved, and to be the person I wanted to be, I couldn't be around them anymore. They couldn't be a part of my life because unhappiness is a disease and it poisons everything. I feel it when I'm around them. It's an invisible hand crawling to me, a phantom's voice beckoning me to return. I can't.

I feel guilty about it, like I should be a big enough person to face them and come out of it whole. I feel like I should be around them, helping in any way I can. I feel like I should be a presence of positivity for them rather than just another source of anger and resentment they use to fuel their noxious decisions.

But I also know what they do to my mental state and well-being. I know what that world does to me, how it messes with my mind, and how that noise drowns out the beauty all around me. I know it would begin to infect my family, and nothing makes me more fearful than to imagine my son having to deal with even a fraction of what I had to endure. I will do anything to make sure he never knows that world exists as he grows and learns as a child.

I don't have the answers to this problem, not in this book, at least. It would be dishonest to say I feel good about any of my options.

It would be great to be able to tie up my story into a nice, neat bow of closure and contentment, but my life's story isn't done yet, and there are still loose ends. There probably always will be. I think that's just the way lives are, and we have to make peace with it, one way or another.

My relationship with my mom is poor and barely existent. When we talk—if we talk—she tells me a lie. I nod and smile, and it ends. My father is nowhere to be seen. My sister is living on disability with some man, and her children, who were with my mother, are now living with other relatives after Child Protective Services was called, yet again. One brother is missing in action, but the other is doing well, and I'm proud of his accomplishments.

I don't know where any of these plot threads will be in a few months, let alone a few years, but I know I will keep pushing on, because enduring is the only real choice I've ever had. All the suffering I made it through and all of the terrible nights I spent wondering why my life was the way it was gave me endurance. My endurance of that pain and suffering built the foundation of my character. My character has fueled every ounce of hope that allows me to try something new, push to the next level, and believe in my students with every fiber of my being.

My hope is my foundation, my strength, and my pride. It is my will to keep going and my light in the dark.

My hope drove me to have the best fourth year in education I could have ever imagined. It drove me to be the best teacher I've ever been. It drove me to be the best dad, husband, citizen, explorer, thinker, and dreamer I could have ever seen myself becoming, and it keeps driving me to get better. I'm not close to perfect, but I am improving.

Hope helps me make this life worth it, and it keeps me from being just another soul lost to circumstance or a victim still scarred from a childhood filled with drugs and violence.

I do not end this book with easy conclusions about my life but with a promise of one final lesson. It's a lesson I learned through experience and one I hope you take to heart, because it can literally change the course of a child's life.

Teach

Teach the students who want to be in your classroom, and teach the students who don't want to be in your classroom.

Teach the students who follow every rule and procedure, and teach the students who never follow any direction.

Teach the children who have more than enough food and security at home, and teach the children who don't know if they'll eat tonight.

Teach the students who stand up and speak proudly, and teach the kids who hide, resist, and complain when you make them use their voices to demonstrate their learning.

Teach the students who have manners, and teach the students who can't even spell the word.

Teach the students who are happy every day, and teach the students who haven't smiled all year, despite your best efforts.

Teach the students who crave more knowledge, and teach the kids who crave to be seen any way they can.

Teach the students who will return to a home filled with love and understanding, and teach the students who will return to homes filled with fear and stress.

Teach.

Teach.

Teach.

Then maybe, just maybe, you will impact a student in a positive way. Maybe you will break the cycle of poverty, suffering, drugs, violence, neglect, low self-esteem, and unimaginable pain and loss. Maybe you'll be the teacher they look back on and thank for igniting the passion they have in their lives.

So teach.

And teach.

And teach.

And teach.

Acknowledgments

To my wife, Kailey: You're the most amazing person I've ever met and are a constant reminder to me of how lucky I am. You understand me more than anyone on the planet, and marrying you is the single best decision I ever made. You have built a life with me, and I couldn't be happier with how it has all worked out so far. Plus, my classroom would look terribly ugly without your help. I love you.

To my son, Maddy: Your excitement about the small things in life, your ability to make anyone laugh and smile, and your endless energy to play and have fun bring me more joy than I could ever possibly describe here. Just by being alive, you make me a better person. I love you.

To my lifelong mentor and friend, Staci Hammer: You were the single best teacher I had and continue to be today. Thank you for always being just a phone call away. Your input and friendship mean the world to me. You cared for me at a time when most of the adults I knew just wanted to forget about me.

To my teaching mentors and friends, John and Melinda Bolles, Kecia Dennis, and Ross and Kate Nelson: You guys are the best. You helped me when I was terrible, and you help me now that I'm not so terrible. You five are among the most honest and compassionate people I know, and my life is better for knowing you and being a part of your lives.

To my teacher, principal, friend, and colleague, James Whitfield: Without your insight and leadership, I'd be far less than what I am today as a person and an educator. You showed me doors and gave me keys to find my own path. You're invaluable. Truly, the next level is coming, sir!

To the teachers I grew up with in this profession, Katie Warren, Malyn Bannister, Becca Chrietzberg, and Marsha Anderson: You guys are truly rock stars. I've loved learning with all four of you and can't wait to see what the future holds for you all.

To my kindergarten teacher, Mrs. Hernandez: You taught me that other cultures are worth learning about and that everyone has something to offer. You taught with kindness and compassion, and the thought of you still makes me smile every day.

To my third-grade teacher, Mrs. Coffee: You sang to us. You read to us. You smiled and played with us. You made me feel safe in school and made me want to wake up in the morning.

To my fourth-grade teacher, Mrs. Urban: You gave me the tools I needed to deal with my life. You inspired me to write. You set me on a course for the life I have now. Thank you, from the bottom of my heart.

To my fifth-grade teacher, Mr. Hansen: You showed me fantasy fiction and taught me that it was cool to like nerdy things. Your love for learning was infectious and still inspires me today.

To my drum directors and band directors, Kevin McNulty, Evan Blackard, and Bill Watson: You three were father figures to me when I needed it most. Without you, who knows how much trouble I would have found myself in throughout high school. Thanks for dealing with me. I owe each of you.

To the educators who've come on to the *Teach Me, Teacher* podcast: You all have helped me build a platform that teachers can learn from and grow with. Thank you for allowing me a chance to give back to the community that has given and continues to give me so much.

To my friends Forrest Dean and Wesley Albaugh: Without the kindness of you and your families, I wouldn't have had a safe place to be away from my family or, sometimes, even food to eat. You have both been among my most supportive friends ever since that time, and I thank you for it.

To my friend and lifelong nemesis, Evan Godwin: Thank you for reading the many terrible chapters, stories, and other odds and ends I've written over the years. Without you, I'm sure very few people would have ever cared about my writing. Your input was invaluable on this book. Hopefully I'll be able to repay the debt.

To my friends Abe Khadar and Gabriel Wilkey: You're both always there to talk out and talk through ideas that come to mind. Without you both, I know I'd be less.

To the best grandma in the world, Betty Hatfield: You didn't live to read this, but I hope you knew how much your care for me was appreciated. You were one of the best people in my life. Rest easy.

To my aunts, uncles, and cousins: You all let me sleep at your houses, fed me, and drove me away from my home when my family was in an especially bad state. I thank each of you for giving me a place of calm and comfort when I needed it most.

To Dave Burgess and Shelley Burgess: Thank you for believing in my testimony enough to publish it. It means the world to me.

To The Ron Clark Academy: Thank you for inspiring me to fight for what education can be. You have inspired my work in countless ways, and I am forever grateful.

To you, the reader: Thank you for reading my story and the stories I've shared about others. I believe all we have in the end is our testimonies, and they all deserve to be heard. I can't wait to hear yours.

Bibliography

Lesson 3: You Have a Purpose

Carver-Thomas, Desiree and Linda Darling-Hammond. *Teacher Turnover: Why It Matters and What We Can Do About It.* Learning Policy Institute, 2017. Available at: learningpolicyinstitute.org/sites/default/files/product-files/Teacher_Turnover_REPORT.pdf.

Lesson 6: Be the Camera in the Room

Dion, Celine. "My Heart Will Go On." Recorded on May 22, 1997. Track 14 on *Titanic: Music from the Motion Picture.* Sony Classical, 1997, compact disc.

Lesson 10: Take the Road Less Traveled

Nadworny, Elissa. "Why Is Undergraduate College Enrollment Declining?" NPR, May 25, 2018. npr.org/2018/05/25/614315950/why-is-undergraduate-college-enrollment-declining

Jones, Jeffrey M. "More U.S. College Students Say Campus Climate Deters Speech." Gallup, March 12, 2018. news.gallup.com/poll/229085/college-students-say-campus-climate-deters-speech.aspx

"Student Debt Viewed as Major Problem; Financial Considerations Important Factor for Most Millennials When Considering Whether to Pursue College." Harvard Keenedy School, 2019. iop.harvard.edu/

student-debt-viewed-major-problem-financial-considerations-important-factor-most-millennials-when

Lesson 14: Books Are Powerful

Miller, Donalyn. *The Book Whisperer: Awakening the Inner Reader in Every Child*. San Francisco: Jossey-Bass, 2009.

Gallagher, Kelly. *Readicide: How Schools Are Killing Reading and What You Can Do About It*. Portsmouth, NH: Stenhouse, 2009.

Lesson 15: Continuous Effort Drives Exponential Gain

Nesloney, Todd and Adam Welcome. *Kids Deserve It: Pushing Boundaries and Challenging Conventional Thinking*. San Diego: Dave Burgess Consulting, 2016.

Lesson 17: Doubt Is a Tool for Reflection

Campbell, Joseph. *The Hero with a Thousand Faces*. San Francisco: New World Library, 2008.

More from
☠ Dave Burgess
Consulting, inc.

Since 2012, DBCI has been publishing books that inspire and equip educators to be their best. For more information on our DBCI titles or to purchase bulk orders for your school, district, or book study, visit **DaveBurgessConsulting.com/DBCIBooks**.

More from the *Like a PIRATE*™ Series

Teach Like a PIRATE by Dave Burgess

eXPlore Like a Pirate by Michael Matera

Learn Like a Pirate by Paul Solarz

Play Like a Pirate by Quinn Rollins

Run Like a Pirate by Adam Welcome

Lead Like a PIRATE™ Series

Lead Like a PIRATE by Shelley Burgess and Beth Houf

Balance Like a Pirate by Jessica Cabeen, Jessica Johnson, and Sarah Johnson

Lead beyond Your Title by Nili Bartley

Lead with Culture by Jay Billy

Lead with Literacy by Mandy Ellis

Leadership & School Culture

Culturize by Jimmy Casas

Escaping the School Leader's Dunk Tank by Rebecca Coda and Rick Jetter

From Teacher to Leader by Starr Sackstein

The Innovator's Mindset by George Couros

Kids Deserve It! by Todd Nesloney and Adam Welcome

Let Them Speak by Rebecca Coda and Rick Jetter

The Limitless School by Abe Hege and Adam Dovico

The Pepper Effect by Sean Gaillard

The Principled Principal by Jeffrey Zoul and
  Anthony McConnell

Relentless by Hamish Brewer

The Secret Solution by Todd Whitaker, Sam Miller, and
  Ryan Donlan

Start. Right. Now. by Todd Whitaker, Jeffrey Zoul, and
  Jimmy Casas

Stop. Right. Now. by Jimmy Casas and Jeffrey Zoul

Unmapped Potential by Julie Hasson and Missy Lennard

They Call Me "Mr. De" by Frank DeAngelis

Your School Rocks by Ryan McLane and Eric Lowe

Technology & Tools

50 Things You Can Do with Google Classroom by Alice Keeler
  and Libbi Miller

50 Things to Go Further with Google Classroom by Alice Keeler
  and Libbi Miller

140 Twitter Tips for Educators by Brad Currie, Billy Krakower,
  and Scott Rocco

Block Breaker by Brian Aspinall

Code Breaker by Brian Aspinall

Google Apps for Littles by Christine Pinto and Alice Keeler

Master the Media by Julie Smith

Shake Up Learning by Kasey Bell

Social LEADia by Jennifer Casa-Todd

Teaching Math with Google Apps by Alice Keeler and
 Diana Herrington

Teachingland by Amanda Fox and Mary Ellen Weeks

Teaching Methods & Materials

All 4s and 5s by Andrew Sharos

The Classroom Chef by John Stevens and Matt Vaudrey

Ditch That Homework by Matt Miller and Alice Keeler

Ditch That Textbook by Matt Miller

Don't Ditch That Tech by Matt Miller, Nate Ridgway, and
 Angelia Ridgway

EDrenaline Rush by John Meehan

Educated by Design by Michael Cohen, The Tech Rabbi

The EduProtocol Field Guide by Marlena Hebern and
 Jon Corippo

Instant Relevance by Denis Sheeran

LAUNCH by John Spencer and A.J. Juliani

Make Learning MAGICAL by Tisha Richmond

Pure Genius by Don Wettrick

The Revolution by Darren Ellwein and Derek McCoy

Shift This! by Joy Kirr

Spark Learning by Ramsey Musallam

Sparks in the Dark by Travis Crowder and Todd Nesloney

Table Talk Math by John Stevens

The Wild Card by Hope and Wade King

The Writing on the Classroom Wall by Steve Wyborney

Inspiration, Professional Growth & Personal Development

Be REAL by Tara Martin

Be the One for Kids by Ryan Sheehy

Creatively Productive by Lisa Johnson

The EduNinja Mindset by Jennifer Burdis

Empower Our Girls by Lynmara Colón and Adam Welcome

The Four O'Clock Faculty by Rich Czyz

How Much Water Do We Have? by Pete and Kris Nunweiler

P Is for Pirate by Dave and Shelley Burgess

A Passion for Kindness by Tamara Letter

The Path to Serendipity by Allyson Apsey

Sanctuaries by Dan Tricarico

Shattering the Perfect Teacher Myth by Aaron Hogan

Stories from Webb by Todd Nesloney

Talk to Me by Kim Bearden

The Zen Teacher by Dan Tricarico

Through the Lens of Serendipity by Allyson Apsey

Children's Books

Beyond Us by Aaron Polansky

Dolphins in Trees by Aaron Polansky

The Princes of Serendip by Allyson Apsey

I Want to Be a Lot by Ashley Savage

Zom-Be a Design Thinker by Amanda Fox

Keynotes and Talks
by Jacob Chastain

I love nothing more than speaking to educators and students across the world. Through my work with the *Teach Me, Teacher* podcast, I've come into contact with hundreds of thousands of educators around the world digitally, but I'd love to come to where you are and speak in person, sharing my thoughts, experiences, and passion for education with your team, event, campus, or district.

Below are the keynotes and talks I offer. If you have something else in mind for me to be a part of that isn't listed here, feel free to reach out and ask! I love collaborating on great ideas.

Let It Rain

Throughout my life, teachers were the rocks I clung to as the storm of my family raged around me. This talk covers my life and key events that shaped me as a person. This talk is my testimony to the power of teachers in the lives of students who've dealt with trauma, and is designed to refocus staff on their *why* and re-energize them for the hard and meaningful work ahead in their classrooms.

Embrace Firsts

I was a terrible teacher my first year, but I learned a lot by embracing firsts and reflecting as often as I could. This talk is a fun and energetic way to get us in the right mindset for a new year, new semester, or even a new idea we want to take into our schools or classrooms. We should love embracing firsts, because it's the only way we will ever get to seconds and thirds.

Take Care of Others

Because of the addictions in my family, I saw first hand what it's like to experience suffering at the hands of others. I lived in fear and anger throughout my childhood and teenage years, until I remembered a moment in my life that showed me that caring for others is the antidote to suffering. This talk is meant to be a reality check for teachers about their roles in students' lives and the lives of their colleagues, and how destructive or empowering they can be.

Books Are Powerful

When my family fell apart, books kept me company. I read voraciously, and found worlds that not only transported me to new lands, but to new ideas and beliefs. This fact has lead me to advocate for authentic reading practices in our classrooms, and this talk will address why we should be filling our students' lives with great and diverse books, and address how to go about that in a meaningful way, without killing the love for reading!

For speaking inquiries, reach me through the contact page at TeachMeTeacherPodCast.com.

About the Author

Jacob Chastain is the host and creator of the *Teach Me, Teacher* podcast, a former literacy coach, and is currently teaching sixth-grade English in Ft. Worth, Texas. He is also slide certified from the Ron Clark Academy.

Jacob believes that educators should be pushing the boundaries of what it means to engage students in the classroom, and that teachers are currently in the golden age of education. With the advent of social media platforms like Instagram, Facebook, and Twitter, educators all over the world can connect and share ideas to improve their craft.

His *Teach Me, Teacher* podcast reaches thousands of educators every month, is a top rated podcast on iTunes, and has featured some of the top minds and personalities in education on the show, such as Donalyn Miller, Penny Kittle, Kim Bearden, and Joe Dombrowski (Mr. D). The show covers anything and everything related to the wonderful world of education, but is sure to focus on how teachers can all step up and be a positive influence for good in their students' lives.

When he is not teaching or podcasting, he's working on his double master's in curriculum and instruction and administrative leadership, playing video games with his son, and browsing bookstores with his wife.

Teach Me, Teacher is his first book for educators, but it is not his last.

If you'd like to follow Jacob, visit
TeachMeTeacherPodCast.com,
or find him on social media.

f   Facebook.com/teachmeteacher

◎   @teachmeteacherhost

▸   @jacobchastain_

Made in the USA
Monee, IL
08 September 2020